The Crystal GUIDE

IDENTIFICATION, PURPOSE, POWERS and VALUES

PATTI POLK

Krause Publications
An imprint of Penguin Random House LLC
penguinrandomhouse.com

ISBN 978-1-4402-4718-7

Printed in Mexico
3   5   7   9   10   8   6   4   2

Cover photographs provided by the author.

Cover design by Sharon Bartsch
Designed by Dane Royer
Edited by Kristine Manty

Contents

Acknowledgments

My deepest appreciation to all of the following people who so generously contributed their photos, expertise, time, and personal collections for me to photograph, without whom this book could not have been written.

Amir Chossrow Akhavan, Kevin Burgart, Barbara Grill, Travis Hartins, William Horton, Mike Keim, Kevin Kessler, Klaus Klement, Yoshihiro Kobayashi, Steve Kluck, Dr. Robert Lavinsky, Lamont Latham, Larry Michon, Dick Moore, Suzanne Morrison, Stacie Hirsch Nutter, Ray Pohlkotte, Trina's Rock Shop, Jim Van Wert, and Chris Whitney-Smith.

Thank you to Haley Allatorre for all her assistance with the editing of the descriptive portions in this book, and an extra big thank you to Paul Kennedy for being such a top-notch book editor and all-around good guy.

All my love to my incredible daughter, Sharon Gardner, and to my favorite son-in-law, Jeff Gardner, for their endless love and support.

And last but not least, the most special thank you to the best man in the whole world, my wonderful husband, Kevin, who truly makes all things possible.

If I have forgotten anyone, I sincerely apologize and will catch you on the next go round!

Quartz crystal with spessartine garnets.
Photo courtesy of Patti Polk.

Introduction

Welcome to the beautiful and fascinating world of crystal minerals. I myself am an avid collector of rocks and minerals, especially the crystalline types. I collect them as specimens for their beauty, to decorate my surroundings, wear them as jewelry, and I use them in holistic practices such as in pendulum dowsing or as protective stones that I carry with me as I travel. I have loved all types of stones since I was a child, just as many children naturally do.

The crystal kingdom is a magical place, full of wonder, mystery, and beauty just waiting to be explored and discovered. To me, there is nothing more joyous than to be out in nature with the warm sunshine, chirping birds, darting lizards, fresh air, and silent landscapes as my companions as I explore Mother Earth, hoping to find just a few of her miraculous buried treasures—the ever-elusive sparkling crystal or shining gemstone. It is truly some of the happiest, and most peaceful, moments in my life. When I am out collecting in the field I am mindful of how precious our Earth is, and I am careful to respect Her by not harming any of Her creatures or wantonly disturbing Her ground. If I do dig out any stones, then I am careful to fill in any holes that I have created and leave the area as I found it. This is always good etiquette for any rock collector or miner.

In choosing to take on the adventure of writing a book about crystals and their uses, I knew that I wanted to write something that was not only helpful and educational for the beginning mineral collector, but would be useful to more experienced collectors, too. I wanted to bridge the worlds between the more traditional, scientific aspects of mineral collecting as display or academic specimens with the more informal nature of how minerals, crystals in particular, are used in other, more holistic, ways. I can appreciate both disciplines, as I am a practitioner of both. I not only have a fairly large mineral specimen collection that I have personally amassed over many years, but I also have quite a collection of special gemstone jewelry and crystals that I use regularly for more arcane purposes. In the Crystal Catalog section of this book, I have

Clear quartz crystal pendulum. Photo courtesy of Patti Polk.

The author beside an amethyst geode for sale at the world-renown Tucson
Gem & Mineral Show in Tucson, Arizona. Photo courtesy of Barbara Grill.

alphabetically listed many of the most popular minerals that people are likely to collect when forming a mineral collection or when seeking crystals that will be useful in their metaphysical practices. Along with their geologic or physical characteristics I have listed some of their esoteric meanings as well. I have focused on adhering to the definition of "crystals" as minerals that generally have a recognizable, visible crystal or *macrocrystalline*, structure as opposed to the fine-grained or *microcrystalline* types, such as the agates, jaspers, cherts, and obsidians that are more solid or compact in structure and don't exhibit obvious crystal forms to the naked eye.

In writing this book, my greatest hope is that any person who is interested in learning about minerals and crystals will find some kind of useful nuggets of information within these pages and be encouraged to investigate the beautiful and enchanting realm of the mineral kingdom with enthusiasm and open-mindedness. Collecting crystals is a rewarding and pleasurable journey, filled with the excitement of discovery and adventure that takes us away from the mundane aspects of our everyday lives and transports us into the exotic and mysterious world that can only be found through personal communion with Mother Earth.

Crystallized specimen of azurite hand-collected in Arizona. Photo courtesy of Patti Polk.

Collecting Crystals

Mankind has been collecting minerals since the first caveman hand-painted red and yellow ochre on the walls of his cave as artful decoration, or to impart important cultural information to his fellow cave dwellers. Minerals, especially crystals, have been used as items of great spiritual significance and as powerful personal adornments for millennia. Minerals, which include metals, crystals, and gemstones, have a long and important history of use in civilization and society. Metallurgy has been practiced for thousands of years with discoveries of mines and furnaces used for smelting copper dating back as far as 5,000 BC. The advent of the discovery of copper and other metals made the Copper and Bronze Ages possible, and with those discoveries came an enormous acceleration in the development of civilization as we know it. Quartz crystals are associated with human funerary rituals dating back from at least the Lower Paleolithic era and quartz tools and numerous pieces of quartz crystal were found with the remains of 'Peking Man' (c. 500,000 B.C) in Beijing, China.

A crystal and mineral collecting book from 1946.

Throughout history, gemstones such as rubies, sapphires, diamonds, and others have always held a special allure for people of all denominations and creeds, and have been coveted and fought over for thousands of years, even to this day. Quartz crystal, in particular, has found innumerable uses since ancient times for such varied purposes as a personal or ritual talisman, healing stone, fortune-teller (as a crystal ball), as a cut and polished gemstone or as carved decorative ornaments, and in more recent times as a conductor and amplifier of electric energy. Due to its piezoelectric properties, quartz crystal has many commercial and industrial uses such as an oscillator used in the timing of clocks and watches, and as a transmitter in the production of radios and modern communication devices. Regardless of how they're used, the study of crystals is certainly a fascinating and enduring subject.

In this book, we are focusing primarily on the collecting and use of the *macrocrystalline* forms of minerals. In other words, minerals that have the form of a recognizable crystal shape. Minerals take many shapes and forms, such as round, bubbly, flat, furry, hair-like, scaly, pointy, powdery, wiry, in sheets, massive, or flower-like, and then there's the structural type that we more commonly encounter in our everyday life - the prism-shaped, elongated, pointed or spikey kind that we generally see

Clockwise from top left: A group of collectors digging for amethyst crystals at Scuffin Acres Farm in Virginia; amethyst crystals in situ at Scuffin Acres Farm; heavy equipment used to open up the ground for crystal digging; Scuffin Acres Farm amethyst crystals after cleaning. Photos courtesy of Larry Michon.

Blue barite crystals with calcite
cluster from Colorado, USA.
Photo courtesy of Patti Polk collection.

as a single crystal or as a cluster of many individuals. These are the type of crystals that
we will be concentrating on here.

So, why do people collect crystals? Well, there are a variety of reasons. For mineral
collectors it is usually for their beauty, rarity, or special features such as having
fluorescence or a certain type of physical formation. Other people collect crystals
because it's fun or because they're pretty and they like to display them for aesthetic
reasons; some people collect them for study or research, and many others collect them
for specific purposes such as using them as tools in metaphysical or healing practices.
Whatever your reason for collecting crystals is—for fun, profit, education, or to use
in helping others—if you want to acquire them, then you need to know where to find
them. Whether you buy them at a rock shop, metaphysical store, at a website online,
at a gem and mineral show, or choose to go dig them yourself in the field, there are a
number of choices you must make in order to obtain what you're looking for. Are you
interested in just buying one for yourself as an attractive display piece, or as a nice gift
for someone else to enjoy? Are you looking to start a serious mineral collection or to
find special pieces with qualities that can be used as healing stones? If you just want to
buy pieces purely for ornamental purposes, then it is a fairly straightforward process to
find what you're looking for. You need only look for a crystal that is pleasing to your
eye, and they can generally be easily found in stores that carry decorative or gift items,
both online or at larger shopping malls. If you want to start a serious mineral collection
or begin a healing practice using gemstones, then there is much more footwork to do.

Smoky quartz crystal polished wand with mineral inclusions. Photo courtesy of Patti Polk.

Single zincite crystal, backlit. Photo courtesy of Patti Polk.

If you are just starting out and want to begin to put together a mineral collection, you will need to learn about the different types of minerals and what their features are. There are many resources available for this such as books about mineral collecting and identification, local gem and mineral clubs, gem and mineral shows, and a variety of informative and educational mineral collecting websites online with easily accessible pictures and information about all types of minerals and crystal formations. Many of these websites also sell minerals so they are a good place to start, especially if you're eager to start buying specimens to add to your collection. If you want to try your hand at field collecting your own crystal specimens, then you will need to learn about what is involved in field collecting. Field collecting usually involves some understanding of the geology of your chosen area, the ability to do a certain amount of hiking, and

A woman standing near a large quartz crystal cluster at the world-famous Tucson, Arizona, Gem and Mineral Show. Photo courtesy of Patti Polk.

physical stamina for digging that may require the use of digging tools such as a small shovel, mattock, prybar, three-prong hand rake, and screwdriver for *gently* prying out your crystals from the host rock. You will also need gloves, a small bottle of water and toothbrush for rinsing and cleaning your specimens, and some kind of container to carry them out. If they are small and delicate, you can wrap them in tissue paper and put them in an egg carton for safe transportation. There are locations in every state in the USA where you can find some kind of minerals to collect and there are many books written specifically about where to collect rocks and minerals that you can get at most bookstores or through online booksellers. Fee-digging sites where you can pay for a day of digging crystals are also available in many places throughout the U.S. and there are a number of them listed in the resource section of this book.

If you are interested in acquiring crystals for use in metaphysical or healing practices, you will need to have an understanding of what kinds of crystals are appropriate to use, how to use them, and what their specific healing properties are. Just as with mineral specimen collecting, there are a multitude of resources available to you on this subject including numerous books on the properties and meaning of crystals,

Rose quartz pendant with chakra stones.
Photo courtesy of Patti Polk.

certified classes in healing techniques, and metaphysical stores both locally and online for purchasing all varieties of mineral and crystal supplies.

One of the most fun ways to learn about, and experience first-hand, the astounding and beautiful world of minerals and crystals is to attend a gem and mineral show. Gem and mineral shows are often held annually by a local gem and mineral club and offer a dazzling array of collectible rocks, gems, crystals, and minerals to peruse and purchase. One of the largest and most spectacular gem and mineral shows in the world takes place yearly in the USA during the months of January through February in Tucson, Arizona, where you can see, touch, and buy crystals weighing from mere ounces up to hundreds of pounds. If you are a bona fide crystal collector it is an experience not to be missed!

Geology and Formation of Crystals

Geology is the science that deals with the earth's physical structure and substance, its history, and the processes that act on it. Geology explains the basic primary forces and functions of Earth that create all the different kinds of rocks, minerals, and crystals that exist in our world. It is important to know at least a little bit about geology if you are interested in collecting crystals and minerals so that you can be somewhat knowledgeable about their classification, form, and composition, especially if you are considering looking for them yourself in the field or earnestly building a well-developed mineral collection.

Geologic Groups

Geology classifies rocks in three main groups, according to the particular Earth processes that formed them. The three rock groups are *igneous, sedimentary,* and *metamorphic* rocks. If you are interested in collecting crystals and minerals you need to become familiar with the characteristics of these three rock groups. It is within these basic groups that all the mineral and crystal specimens that you are looking for will be found.

Hillsides covered in volcanic rock (igneous). Photo courtesy of Patti Polk.

Cliffs showing layered iron-rich sedimentary rocks. Photo courtesy of Patti Polk.

Igneous rocks are formed from melted rock or *magma* that has cooled and solidified. Due to high pressure and temperature, rocks that are buried deep within the Earth become superheated and melt, and the molten rock then flows upward through fissures in the Earth's mantle or is erupted from a volcano onto the Earth's surface. When the magma cools deep within the Earth, crystals grow slowly from the cooling molten liquid, and a coarse-grained (*macrocrystalline*) rock forms. When the magma cools rapidly, usually at or near the Earth's surface, the crystals form quickly and are very tiny, creating a fine-grained (*microcrystalline*) rock. Large bodies of igneous plutonic coarse-grained rock called pegmatites are often the source of some of the world's finest gemstones, such as beryl or tourmaline.

Sedimentary rocks are formed at or near the surface of the Earth, either in wet environments or on land. Sedimentary rocks are layered accumulations of sediments, such as fragments of rocks, minerals, sands, or the remnants of animal and plant matter that become cemented together by chemicals and minerals over time through low temperatures and pressures that harden them into new, compacted forms like shale or sandstone.

When sedimentary and igneous rocks are subjected to pressures so intense or heat so high that they are completely transformed, they become *metamorphic rocks*. The processes of metamorphism changes the primary rock into denser, more compact rocks that can then develop into an entirely new and different type of rock. New minerals

An example of gneiss, a metamorphic rock. Photo courtesy of Patti Polk.

are also created within the rock either by alteration of the existing internal mineral components or by reactions with additional chemical fluids that enter and modify the original rocks.

All of the collectible minerals and crystals that we are interested in for our purposes can be found within these three groups. Many are found within the igneous group, others are found in the sedimentary or metamorphic groups.

Minerals, especially the macrocrystalline (visible crystal structure) type, exhibit a variety of characteristics that can be used to recognize and to categorize them, such as their mineral classification, crystal system, habit, or other identifying information. One of the most common ways of immediately beginning to identify a mineral in hand is by observation of its physical properties and asking a few simple questions. What is its shape and color? Is it shiny or dull, transparent or opaque, and does it exhibit a particular crystal habit? Is it heavy or metallic? What color streak does it leave on a streak plate? Does it fluoresce or is it magnetic?

One of the best ways of assessing the type of a crystal is by testing its hardness. There is a scale of hardness called the Mohs scale that can tell you the hardness of a crystal by using a series of scratch tests that give a numerical value of how hard they are. The higher the number, the harder the material, all the way up to diamond, the hardest of all. For example, if specimen A can scratch Specimen B, then Specimen A is harder than Specimen B. If specimen A does not scratch Specimen B, then Specimen B is harder than

Specimen A. It is important to know this because it will help you to determine what kind of crystal you have since many crystals look similar but may vary a great deal in hardness depending on what their mineral composition is. Also, if you intend to handle a crystal regularly or to use it in a piece of jewelry, you want to be sure that it is of a sufficient hardness to stand up to its intended use. Most minerals under the hardness of 5 tend to be too soft or fragile for prolonged use or heavy handling.

Mohs Hardness Scale

SCALE	MINERAL	SCRATCH TEST
1	Talc	Fingernail
2	Gypsum	Fingernail
3	Calcite	Copper penny
4	Fluorite	Metal nail
5	Apatite	Knife blade
6	Feldspar	Steel file
7	Quartz	Masonry drill bit
8	Topaz	Masonry drill bit
9	Corundum	Diamond drill bit
10	Diamond	Diamond

To be able to accurately identify minerals, it is also important to know the classification of the type of mineral species you are dealing with. The most commonly used system is known as the Dana Classification system, with an abbreviated version shown below. There are a variety of chemical or heating tests that can be performed to accurately determine the composition of mineral specimens, but these are usually best left to the professionals.

Mineral Classifications

NATIVE ELEMENTS	Native Elements
SULFIDES	Includes selenides, tellurides, sulfosalts
OXIDES AND HYDROXIDES	Simple oxides, hydroxides, multiple oxides
HALIDES	Anhydrous and hydrated halides, oxyhalides, hydroxyhalides, halide complexes, compound halides
CARBONATES, NITRATES, AND BORATES	Includes carbonates, nitrates, and borates
SULFATES, CHROMATES, SELENATES	Includes sulfates, chromates, selenates, and tellurates
PHOSPHATES, ARSENATES, AND VANADATES	Includes phosphates, antimonites, arsenites, phosphites, vanadium oxysalts, anhydrous molybdates and tungstates
ORGANIC MINERALS	Salts of organic acids and hydrocarbons
SILICATES	Neosilicates, sorosilicates, cyclosilicates, inosilicates, phyllosilicates, tektosilicates

Rutilated quartz crystal polished sphere.
Photo courtesy of Patti Polk.

Next, it is good to know the manner of *crystallization*, or the visible external form of the symmetry of the crystal's structure.

Crystal Forms

SYSTEM	AXIS	FORM
ISOMETRIC (or cubic)	Three axes of symmetry, all at right angles to one another and all of equal length.	
HEXAGONAL	Four axes of symmetry, three of equal length lie in a plane at 120`, the fourth axis is of unequal size at right angles to the others.	
TETRAGONAL	Three axes of symmetry, two axes of equal length lie in a plane at 90`, the third is of unequal size at right angles to the others.	
ORTHORHOMBIC	Three unequal axes, all at right angels to each other.	
MONOCLINIC	Three unequal axes, two axes at right angels to each other on a plane, the third axis is inclined to the plane of the other two, and one twofold axis.	
TRICLINIC	Three axes, all of unequal lengths and none perpendicular to the others.	

And, last but not least, the habit of the mineral – its characteristic shape and appearance, as defined by the form of its growth and its relative proportions.

There are many different mineral habits, and included here are the most commonly used in identifying collectible mineral specimens, with additional definitions included in the glossary.

Crystal Habits

HABIT	DESCRIPTION
ACICULAR	Needlelike or hair-like.
AGGREGATES	Made of numerous crystals or clusters.
BLADED	Aggregates of thin, tabular crystals.
BLOCKY	The crystal shape tends to be equant, chunky or squarish.
BOTRYOIDAL	Bubbly or grape-like, globular. Usually a surface coating.
CAPILLARY	Very thin and long, like a thread or hair.
COLUMNAR	Crystals in the shape of parallel columns.
COMB OR COXCOMB	Layers on top of each other that produce a toothed structure.
CUBIC	Crystals shaped like cubes.
CRUCIFORM	Twinned tabular crystals with a cross-like outline.
DENDRITIC	Treelike or branching patterns.
DISSEMINATED	Occuring as small, distinct particles dispersed in matrix.
DRUSE OR DRUZE	Fine surface coating of tiny crystals.
EQUANT	Having similar diameter in all directions. Square.
FAN-SHAPED	Crystallization shaped like a fan.

HABIT	DESCRIPTION
FIBROUS	Crystals formed of fibers.
FOLIATED	Two-dimensional platy forms.
GLOBULAR	Spherical, bubble-like, rounded forms.
GRANULAR	Grainy, or having grains.
INCLUSIONS	Fragments of minerals included with another mineral.
MASSIVE	Containing dense, interlocked crystalline grains. Amorphous, without a definitive shape.
MICAEOUS	Thin, flexible, flat sheets like pages of a book, mica-like.
OOLITIC	Filled with small spheres.
PLATY	In sheets or plate-like forms.
PRISMATIC	Prismatic crystals typically having 3, 4, 6, 8 or 12 faces that are parallel to a crystallographic axis.
PYRAMIDAL	Crystals shaped like pyramids.
RADIATING	Crystals growing outward from a center point.
RENIFORM	Kidney-shaped.
ROSETTE	Crystal aggregate shaped like a rose.
SCALY	Exhibiting scales, like a fish.
STRIATED	Parallel grooves on crystal faces.
STALACTITIC	Elongated, columnar shaped formations. Like stalactites.
STELLATE	Spherical aggregates radiating from a star-like center point.
STUBBY	Short or squat, thick crystals.
TABULAR	Flat, square, or rectangular planes, wider in one direction.
WHEAT-SHEAF	Similar to a bundle of straw, hourglass-shaped.

Use and Care of Crystal Specimens

There are a great variety of uses for the minerals and crystals we collect. For many people it is simply a matter of having beautiful and interesting decorative pieces to adorn their environment, while others might want to use them to cut and polish for jewelry making. Other people may want to accumulate a specific type of crystal or mineral to create a personal mineral collection, and others may choose to use them as important tools in healing practices or for ceremonial purposes. Whatever your particular interest is, there is an abundance of information available to you about how to go about utilizing and caring for your crystals and minerals. If your interest is in using stones to set in jewelry there are many excellent books and classes online or local community classes to learn how to do lapidary work (the art of cutting and polishing stones), and working with metals (silversmithing, goldsmithing and wire-wrapping).

Building a Collection

If your interest is in building a personal mineral collection for yourself, then there are definitely a few things to consider before you begin acquiring specimens in earnest. What are your reasons for collecting? Is it because it's fun, a favorite passion, or the thrill of the hunt? Or, do you enjoy the science behind the minerals – their chemistry, mineralogy, the geological settings that they form in, or the mineral associations that they form together? Do you like the challenge of finding the perfect specimen—one that combines all the elements of a specific species—its rarity, location, size, color, aesthetic, and at a good price?

Tourmalinated quartz ring.
Photo courtesy of Patti Polk.

What do you consider a great specimen? Sometimes this is a difficult question to answer. There are so many factors that contribute to what makes up a collectible specimen. Many of the deciding factors are objective, in that they can be measured, but some are subjective, determined by the personal taste and eye of the beholder. However, when collecting or purchasing specimens for your collection, the most important thing to remember is that you, the collector, should really like the specimen regardless of what anyone else thinks. It is your collection and for your enjoyment! When you build your collection yourself mineral by mineral, you are creating something that you can continue to expand upon and enjoy for a lifetime.

The main characteristics that are generally accepted as factors in determining a good quality mineral specimen are first, is the specimen well-crystallized? In other words, does it display an attractive, definitive, and well-structured example of its crystal form? When I say crystal form, that also means specimens that are not only prismatic in shape – but others that may be round, acicular, fibrous, or any other type of structure. Other factors to consider are size, color, rarity, locality, luster and transparency. Also, are there associated desirable or unusual minerals attached to the primary mineral and is the specimen in pristine condition, with no damage or repairs? Additionally, if a specimen is especially aesthetically pleasing due to its exceptional colors or combination of forms, or has an important history or provenance, that too will affect it's desirability (and value).

Crystal Storage, Labeling, and Sizes

Most mineral collectors want to build as comprehensive a collection as possible of whatever their chosen type of collectible mineral is. Whether you choose to collect *micromounts* (very small, perfect specimens of all kinds), fluorescent minerals, or only minerals of certain colors, shapes, or species, keep in mind that quality - not just large sizes or quantities, makes for a good collection. Also, many fine minerals don't occur in large sizes and smaller specimens tend to be more affordable. If space is an issue, it can be a real benefit to focus on collecting smaller specimens since a collector can then have far more quality specimens in their collection that can fit in the available space.

To store, protect, and identify mineral specimens, most of the smaller ones are kept in a variety of standard-sized white cardboard boxes or in small plastic boxes that have a transparent lid that can be snapped shut, and labels are then applied to the boxes with the mineral identification information. Cardboard mineral storage boxes usually come with cotton padding in standard sizes of 1" x 1", 1-1/2" x 1-1/2", 2" x 2" and up, and the small plastic ones, called "perky boxes," are a cube measuring 1-1/4" on each side, with a styrofoam insert in the bottom. The perky box will hold a micromount specimen up to 3/4" tall x 3/4" wide. There are also 1" x 1" clear plastic boxes with a built-in magnifying lid for viewing very tiny specimens. The small specimens are held in place in the boxes with a sticky substance called *museum putty*, available through gem and mineral specialty stores.

It is important to have a system of labeling your specimens so they don't get mixed up. Many people paint a small rectangle of white enamel paint on a hidden area of each specimen and number it in black ink. Then the mineral number, mineral name, collector's name, date collected, location and other pertinent data are entered in a small notebook to keep track of the collection.

When it comes to defining the size of mineral specimens there is a generally accepted list of classifications that mineral buyers, sellers, and collectors go by. The categories of the mineral sizes is as follows:

MICROMOUNTS	Specimens when mounted will fit into a 1-1/4" x 1-1/4" perky box, (specimen size up to 3/4" x 3/4").
THUMBNAILS	Specimens that fit into a 1" x 1" cube.
MINIATURES	Specimens that fit into a 2" x 2" cube.
HAND SPECIMENS (or Small cabinet)	Specimens that are over 2" x 2" and under 5" x 5".
CABINET SPECIMENS	Specimens too large to fit into a 5" cube.

These are the sizes we will be using for reference in the Crystal Catalog section.

Care and Cleaning of Specimens

It is also important to know how to take proper care of your mineral specimens and a little bit of understanding of the chemistry of your minerals would be very helpful here. Many minerals have properties that are affected by air, light, heat, moisture, temperature, or by physical contact. In order to protect your mineral specimens you need to know their sensitivities and plan accordingly. For example, amethyst may fade and lose its purple color over time if left in direct sunlight, so you need to be sure to keep it away from the sun. Some minerals are durable enough to be coated with a light film of oil or acrylic spray to seal them from excessive moisture, and some soft minerals must never be directly touched or they will be destroyed due to their fragility.

There are a number of ways to clean and prepare your specimens. If you purchase your specimens from a seller, then they have probably already been cleaned and prepared as well as they can be and may only need an occasional light dusting if they are not too delicate to tolerate it. If you have personally collected

A micromount stibnite mineral specimen in an open perky box.
Photo courtesy of Patti Polk.

A miniature copper mineral specimen in a 1-1/2" x 1-1/2" box. Photo courtesy of Patti Polk.

your specimens in the field or got them from someone else who field-collected them and they haven't been cleaned, then you will need to clean them yourself. The first thing you'll want to do is to carefully trim away any excess matrix from the specimen using a trimming hammer, nippers, pliers, chisels or a lapidary trim saw. Some minerals are too fragile and can't be cleaned at all and must be left as-is. Sometimes a simple rinsing in cool water is enough, providing they aren't water-soluble minerals or so fine as to be damaged by the action of the water. Many specimens may be cleaned in *lukewarm* soapy water by gentle brushing with a toothbrush or paintbrush - be careful not to use water that is too hot or too cold as it may cause some crystals to fracture from shock. You can use dental tools to pick out small pieces of dirt or debris, and a high-pressure water gun can do wonders on removing stubborn stains and encrustations that nothing else will touch. Many stains can also be removed by chemical cleaners such as oxalic or muriatic acid, but be absolutely sure that you know how to handle them if you choose to use those options, as they can be dangerous.

Metaphysical Uses of Crystals

If your interest is in using crystals for metaphysical purposes there are a number of different ways to use them. They can be used as an aid in meditation, divination, or channeling; worn as an amulet for protection or healing, used as a tool in healing yourself or others, as an environmental energy enhancer, cleaner or protector, or as an essence in a gem elixir. No matter how you prefer to use crystals there are certain basic concepts that you will need to know to be competent with their properties and functions. In the Crystal Catalog section of this book, most of the primary uses for each crystal are given with the description of the crystal, along with it's vibrational number, astrological sign, and chakra associations. How you choose to use them is up to you – but, be fearless, be creative, and most of all, enjoy the journey into the marvelous realm of the magical crystal!

If you are new to the world of crystal collecting, you will first need to find a source for the crystals you desire. That may be through a rock shop, a metaphysical or specialty store, a gem and mineral show, through an online retailer, or you may go and dig them yourself in the field. Personally, my favorite way is to dig them myself, but sadly most people just don't have the time and opportunity to be able to go out and dig crystals themselves. Fortunately, there are many terrific avenues to acquire just about any kind of crystal you might want, and at affordable prices too. It is always best if you can personally see and feel any crystal that you want to purchase instead of buying them blindly through an online source because there will be crystals that you will inherently resonate with and be attracted to, and the only way to know that is to experience it first-hand. If you can, you need to be able to hold them in your hand and see what it feels like. Does it make you feel strong, or happy, or calm? Or, does it leave you feeling cold? Is it warm in your hand? Do you feel a connection to it? This is the time to trust your intuition and make your choices depending on what

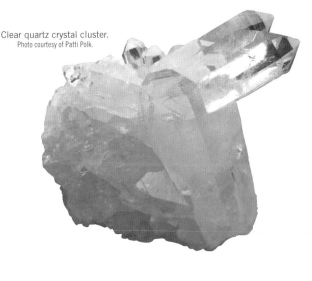

Clear quartz crystal cluster.
Photo courtesy of Patti Polk.

An amethyst pendant with quartz crystal point and sphere. Photo courtesy of Patti Polk.

A bundle of sage used for smudging crystals.
Photo courtesy of Patti Polk.

A healing practitioner's wand made from multiple stones of chakra colors.
Photo courtesy of Patti Polk.

you perceive through your subtle senses.

Once you have chosen the crystal you want, it is a good idea to clear or clean it of unwanted energies. This can be done by rinsing it in clean running water or soaking it in salt water (rinsing afterward with clean water), while mentally holding the intent that all negativity will be washed away and that the crystal will be positively cleaned and charged. A good way of charging crystals is by letting them sit on top of a large quartz crystal cluster overnight, or you can also set crystals in the moonlight or sunlight for a few hours to clear them, but remember that if you leave a crystal in the daylight be sure that it is one whose color won't fade in UV rays. Another good way to clean them is by smudging - using sage or other herbal leaves that are tied together with string into a tight bundle, lighting the bundle on fire, holding it at one end and letting it slowly burn and cleanse the crystal with its smoke. It is also recommended to program your crystals with positive intention such as using positive affirmations to bless them, or to visualize them filled and enveloped in pure white light, which happens to be my favorite way to program them.

Depending on how you want to use your crystals there are a number of ways to utilize them. For healing yourself or others you will want to either place the crystals for a period of time on the appropriate chakra points of the body or hold them in your

Carved and polished
rose quartz heart.
Photo courtesy of Patti Polk.

A dowsing pendulum with smoky
and clear quartz crystals made by
the author. Photo courtesy of Patti Polk.

hand and gently touch, press, rub, or rotate them on the affected parts of the body that need healing while visualizing the necessary treatments, or place them is an area close in proximity to you where they work quietly in the background. You can put them between yourself and harmful electromagnetic energies, such as are emitted from computers or televisions, to help alleviate their effects. You may also want to put them on or around you in meditation to shield from negative energies or to help you focus on your desired goals. Depending on my various needs, I personally like to carry a variety or combination of stones in my pants pocket or in a small pouch around my neck as I go about my business throughout the day.

Crystals, in and of themselves, are benign entities, so you need never worry about causing harm to yourself or others by using crystals with helpful and positive intentions, so don't be afraid to try them out. I do strongly suggest though, if you really want to learn about how to work with crystals in a serious way, then you need to take some classes from an approved instructor and educate yourself as much as possible in their meaning, affinities, and properties. I have included a few basic references in this book to get you started, but this is really just a beginning in the possibilities of what there is to learn about the workings and mysteries of crystal usage.

Pink tourmaline crystal
in lepidolite.
Photo courtesy of Patti Polk.

Crystal Catalog

Mineral Properties

Collectible mineral crystallizations come in a wide variety of shapes, colors and sizes, and can be difficult to distinguish from each other without knowing certain identifying characteristics. Included in this section, along with their photos, are some of the main attributes necessary to identify different minerals by their chemistry, anatomical structure, physical appearance, habit, colors, associated minerals, environment, and other notable features. In some instances, more than one photo may be shown if there are multiple forms of a given mineral.

Also included in this section are descriptions of a variety of metaphysical properties such as particular crystal attributes, astrological and chakra associations, and vibrational numbers that can be used for many different healing practices.

Astrological Properties

Astrology is the study of the movements and positional relationships of celestial objects as a means for divining information about human affairs and earthly events. The use of astrology has been dated to at least the 2nd millennium BCE, and has its roots in calendar systems used to interpret and predict seasonal or celestial cycles. Astrology had its earliest beginnings in ancient Mesopotamia, and has been used by cultures in India, China, and Egypt, as well as the Mayans in the Americas for millennia. Throughout most of its history, astrology was considered a scholarly tradition and was common in academic circles, often in close relation with astronomy, alchemy, meteorology, and medicine.

In astrology, all twelve signs of the zodiac have corresponding crystal affiliations designated by month of birth and the planets associated with their constellations. Below is a chart referencing some of the characteristics used in the art of astrological interpretation as it pertains to the use of crystals and the healing arts.

SIGN	RULES	MODERN CRYSTAL AFFILIATIONS
ARIES ♈ March 21 to April 19	Head and face, the eyes.	Amethyst, Anyolite, Aquamarine, Aventurine, Axinite, Bixbite, Bloodstone, Citrine, Crocoite, Datolite, Diamond, Dravite Tourmaline, Fire Agate, Magnesite, Magnetite, Sardonyx, Sunstone
TAURUS ♉ April 20 to May 20	The neck, ears, throat, larynx, tonsils.	Amber, Amblygonite, Azurite, Carnelian, Diamond, Emerald, Kunzite, Malachite, Plume Agate, Rhodochrosite, Rose Quartz, Selenite, Tourmaline, Turquoise, Variscite

SIGN	RULES	MODERN CRYSTAL AFFILIATIONS
GEMINI ♊ May 21 to June 20	The arms, shoulders, (muscles and bones in these), the lungs, and hands.	Agate, Apophyllite, Aquamarine, Calcite, Celestite, Citrine, Chrysocolla, Emerald, Kyanite, Sapphire, Serpentine, Tanzanite, Thulite, Tourmaline, Ulexite, Variscite, Zoisite
CANCER ♋ June 21 to July 22	Stomach, breasts, solar plexus, diaphragm, upper part of the liver.	Amber, Beryl, Brookite, Calcite, Carnelian, Chalcedony, Citrine, Emerald, Golden Topaz, Natrolite, Opal, Moonstone, Rhodonite, Pearl, Rose Quartz, Ruby
LEO ♌ July 23 to August 22	The heart and spine.	Amber, Aventurine, Carnelian, Citrine, Danburite, Emerald, Garnet, Golden Topaz, Kunzite, Labradorite, Larimar, Muscovite, Peridot, Petalite, Pyrolusite, Rhodochrosite, Ruby, Rutilated Quartz, Sunstone, Tigers Eye, Yellow Sapphire, Zircon
VIRGO ♍ August 23 to September 22	The intestines, alimentary canal, lower part of the liver.	Amazonite, Aquamarine, Azurite, Blue Sapphire, Blue Topaz, Carnelian, Garnet, Gaspeite, Jasper, Lapis Lazuli, Magnetite, Moss Agate, Peridot, Sardonyx, Smithsonite, Turquoise, Zircon
LIBRA ♎ September 23 to October 22	Kidneys, loins, appendix, lumbar vertebrae and the skin generally.	Ametrine, Bloodstone, Chiastolite, Chrysoprase, Citrine, Lapis Lazuli, Lepidolite, Moonstone, Morganite, Opal, Tourmaline, Prehnite, Rose Quartz, Tanzanite, Tourmalinated Quartz
SCORPIO ♏ October 23 to November 21	Reproductive organs, bladder, gall bladder, colon and rectum.	Agate, Boji Stone, Charoite, Dioptase, Golden Topaz, Hiddenite, Kunzite, Labradorite, Malachite, Obsidian, Rhodochrosite, Ruby, Smoky Quartz, Spinel, Tourmalinated Quartz, Turquoise, Variscite
SAGITTARIUS ♐ November 22 to December 21	The hips, thighs and sciatic nerves.	Amethyst, Atacamite, Azurite, Charoite, Dioptase, Herkimer Diamonds, Fluorite, Iolite, Labradorite, Lapis Lazuli, Ruby, Snowflake Obsidian, Sodalite, Tanzanite, Topaz, Turquoise, Vesuvianite, Zircon

SIGN	RULES	MODERN CRYSTAL AFFILIATIONS
CAPRICORN ♑ December 22 to January 19	The knees, joints of the body and the hair.	Agate, Black Onyx, Bloodstone, Chalcopyrite, Fluorite, Galena, Garnet, Hematite, Jet, Magnetite, Malachite, Red Jasper, Schorl Tourmaline, Smoky Quartz, Vesuvianite
AQUARIUS ♒ January 20 to February 18	The lower leg (calves and ankles), the teeth and circulation of the blood.	Amethyst, Angelite, Boji Stone, Clear quartz, Cryolite, Diamond, Garnet, Lithium Quartz, Magnetite, Rainforest Jasper, Sugilite
PISCES ♓ February 19 to March 20	The feet and toes.	Alexandrite, Amethyst, Ametrine, Aquamarine, Azurite, Bloodstone, Blue Lace Agate, Fluorite, Kyanite, Jade, Quartz crystal, Rutilated Quartz, Smithsonite, Turquoise

An open geode with stalactitic and prismatic quartz crystals lining the cavity.
Photo courtesy of Patti Polk.

Chakra Properties

Chakras are part of an ancient medicinal belief system that defines specific energy vortexes in the human body that regulate energy flow within our physical and etheric bodies to promote either well-being or disease depending on their health and balance of energy. In a healthy individual, the chakras are running smoothly, spinning like busy little wheels—but when they fall out of balance, they shut down and don't produce the life force that is necessary to support the health of the region of the body that they are responsible for, resulting in illness. In traditional Hindu belief there are seven major chakras in the body that correspond to the glands in our endocrine system, although in more recent times, a number of new chakras have been discovered. However, for our purposes we will focus on the original seven chakras as they are the primary foundation of the chakra system.

CHAKRA	RULERSHIP	ZODIAC	COLOR	CRYSTAL AFFINITIES
CROWN (7th) Top of head	Spirituality; Upper skull, cerebral cortex, skin	Aquarius	Violet, gold, white	Amethyst, clear quartz, diamond
THIRD EYE (6th) Above & between eyebrows	Intuition, wisdom; Eyes, base of skull	Sagittarius, Pisces	Indigo	Amethyst, fluorite, azurite
THROAT (5th) Middle base of neck	Communication, self-expression; Mouth throat, ears	Gemini, Virgo	Blue	Lapis lazuli, turquoise, aquamarine
HEART (4th) Center of chest	Love & relationships; Heart & chest, lungs, circulation	Libra, Taurus	Green or Pink	Watermelon tourmaline, rose quartz, emerald
SOLAR PLEXUS (3rd) Between navel & base of sternum	Self-will, personal power; Digestive system, muscles	Aries, Leo	Yellow	Aventurine quartz, sunstone, yellow citrine
SACRAL (2nd) Lower abdomen below navel	Sexuality & emotional balance: Sex organs, bladder, prostate, uterus	Cancer, Scorpio	Orange	Citrine, carnelian, golden topaz
ROOT (1st) Between anus & genitals	Survival & physical needs: Bones, skeleton	Capricorn	Red	Hematite, red jasper, bloodstone

Numerical Properties

Numbers also have specific qualities and characteristics associated with them. The study of numbers and their significance is called numerology and has been practiced since mankind first discovered mathematics. To this day, most cultures attach special meaning to certain numbers and their position in a sequence. For example, the ancient Chinese numerical system the I Ching describes the differences between even (earthly) and odd (heavenly) numbers. Numerology has also been used to correlate the significance of numbers to an alphabet, giving each letter a numerical value. A well-known example is the Hebrew alphabet of twenty-two characters, the same as the number of trump cards in the Tarot deck. Because of the applicability of numbers to alphabets, numerologists are able to use words or names, in addition to numbers, to reveal divinatory meaning.

Today, there are three major forms of numerology: the Kabbalic, Chaldean, and Pythagorean. Kabbalic numerology is generally used to interpret names, and is originally derived from Hebrew mysticism, as an outgrowth of the Hebrew alphabet with its twenty-two vibrations. Chaldean numerology has close ties with western astrology and operates on the basis that each letter has a unique vibration and is assigned a number from 1 to 8 based on its energetic quality, except for the number 9. The number 9 is kept separately from the other numbers, except when it appears as a sum of vibrations because it is considered the most sacred number. Pythagorean numerology typically uses both the name and the date of birth, and then examines the relationships between them, much like the Chaldean method. The basic numbers are 1 through 9, with the master numbers 11 and 22, which are never reduced to a single digit as are the other numerical combinations.

NUMBER	MEANING
1	Number 1 resonates with the vibrations and attributes of new beginnings, creation, independence, uniqueness, motivation, progress, ambition and will power, positivity, the energies of pioneering, raw energy, force, activity, self-leadership and assertiveness, initiative, instinct and intuition, the masculine attributes, achievement and success, strength and self-reliance, tenacity, forcefulness and authority, inspiration, attainment, glory, fame, fulfillment, and creating your own realities.
2	Number 2 resonates with the vibrations of service and duty, balance and harmony, adaptability, diplomacy, charm, cooperation, consideration, friendliness, receptivity and love, understanding, peacemaking, gentleness and kindness, art, insightfulness, sensitivity, placidity, justice, sociability, poise, flexibility, grace, devotion, mediation, partnerships and relationships, unions, encouragement, faith and trust, serving others.

NUMBER	MEANING
3	Number 3 resonates with the energies of optimism and joy, inspiration and creativity, speech and communication, good taste, imagination and intelligence, sociability and society, friendliness, kindness and compassion, art, humor, energy, growth, expansion and the principles of increase, spontaneity, broad-minded thinking, encouragement, assistance, talent and skills, culture, wit, a love of fun and pleasure, freedom-seeking, adventure, exuberance, brilliance, courage, rhythm, passion, surprise, self-expression, affability, enthusiasm, youthfulness, psychic ability, manifesting your desires.
4	Number 4 resonates with the vibrations and energies of practicality, organization, service, patience, devotion, application, pragmatism, patriotism, dignity, trust and trust-worthiness, endurance, loyalty, mastery, building solid foundations, conservatism, determination, production and hard work, high morals, traditional values, honesty and integrity, inner strength, security, self-control, loyalty, conscientiousness, being rooted in reality, stability, practical ability, progress, management, seriousness, discipline, system and order, maintenance, constructiveness, dependability, conviction, passion and drive.
5	Number 5 resonates with the influences and attributes of personal freedom, the unconventional, individualism, non-attachment, change, life lessons learned through experience, variety, adaptability and versatility, resourcefulness, motivation, progress, activity, travel and adventure, release and surrender, influence, sensuality, promotion, natural flair, vivacity, courage, idealism, telepathy, pleasure-seeking, vitality, vision, expansion, opportunity, story-telling, mercy, kindness, invention, magnetism, competitiveness, imagination, curiosity, cleverness and intelligence, making life choices and decisions.
6	Number 6 is related to the vibrations and energies of unconditional love, balance and harmony, home and family, domesticity, parenthood, guardianship, service to others, selflessness, responsibility, nurturing, care, empathy and sympathy, self-sacrifice, humanitarianism, the ability to compromise, emotional depth, honesty and integrity, protection, health and healing, idealism, conscientiousness, solution-finding, problem-solving, seeing clearly, teaching, curiosity, peace and peacefulness, simplicity, reliability, material needs and economy, providing and provision, agriculture and growth, musical talent.
7	Number 7 resonates with the vibrations of faith and spirituality, spiritual awakening, awareness, spiritual development and enlightenment, mysticism, intuition, inner-wisdom, psychic abilities, the esoteric, contemplation, introspection, religion, thoughtfulness, secrets, myth, ritual, peace, inner strength, persistence of purpose, the ability to bear hardships, the loner, solitary, isolation, intentions, manifesting reality, good fortune, mental analysis, philosophy, technical knowledge, scientific research, science, alchemy, genius, a keen mind, the specialist, the inventor, determination, the written word, logic, understanding, discernment, knowledge-seeking, study, education and learning, writing and the writer, the ability to set boundaries, refinement, stoicism, silence, seeking perfection, chastity, dignity, the ascetic.

NUMBER	MEANING
8	Number 8 resonates with the influences and vibrations of authority and personal power, self-confidence, executive ability, inner strength, professionalism, achieving and achievements, decisiveness, control, ambition, the authoritarian, management, material freedom, success, using good judgment, money, finances, riches, manifesting wealth, abundance and prosperity, investments, discernment, giving and receiving, thoroughness, dependability, self-reliance, practicality, self-sufficiency, social status, pragmatism, the ego, the executive, delegation, truth and integrity, employment, stability, appearance, customs, skills and talents, exchanges, problem-solving, organizational skills, challenge, efficiency, trustworthiness, insight, planning, working independently, learning through experience, patience, caution, self-discipline, free will, karma.
9	Number 9 is the number of universal love, eternity, faith, spiritual laws, karma, spiritual enlightenment, spiritual awakening, service to humanity, humanitarianism, leading by positive example, philanthropy, charity, self-sacrifice, selflessness, destiny, soul purpose and mission, divine wisdom, mysticism, generosity, a higher perspective, strength of character, public relations, responsibility, intuition, learning to set personal boundaries, creative abilities, sensitivity, loyalty, brilliance, self-love, optimism, freedom, popularity, high ideals, tolerance, humility, altruism and benevolence, empathy, compassion, non-conformity, an expansive viewpoint, eccentricity, communication, influence, perfection, magnetism, understanding, forgiveness, compassion and sympathy, the visionary, duty and calling, obligation.

Rough garnet crystal.
Photo courtesy of Patti Polk.

The Crystals

In this section are included many, but certainly not all, of the minerals and crystals that are considered collectible, nor is every single location listed as to where a certain type of crystal may be found. There are some crystals that are quite unique and may only be found in a few areas worldwide, and then there are others that may occur in hundreds of regions throughout the world. The most important and recognized locations are listed in this section along with approximate retail values to help you with evaluating the purchasing costs of your crystals.

Specimen Pricing

It is important to keep in mind that crystal and mineral prices can fluctuate a great deal depending on many factors, such as mineral desirability and availability, the venue you are purchasing from, and even the part of the country or world where you are doing your buying. The crystal specimens shown in this section range in value from only a few dollars to hundreds or thousands of dollars, depending on the quality, rarity, and desirability of the specimens. The base prices listed in the value chart are a guideline estimating the minimum price that you might reasonably expect to pay for a decent quality example of that specimen through a retail dealer, and the prices go up from there, depending on quality.

Specimen Size References

MICROMOUNTS	Specimens up to 3/4" x 3/4"
THUMBNAILS	Specimens no larger than 1" x 1"
MINIATURES	Specimens no larger than 2" x 2"
SMALL CABINET	Specimens over 2" x 2" and under 5" x 5"
CABINET & LARGER	Specimens larger than 5" x 5"

A

Andalusite

RULES

Root

Third Eye

Andalusite from Austria, small cabinet.
Photo courtesy of Dr. Robert Lavinsky collection.

Andalusite is aluminum silicate and forms as stubby, prismatic crystals, square in cross-section, sometimes in rod-like aggregates. Andalusite is transparent to semi-opaque and has a vitreous luster. The variety *chiastolite* commonly contains dark inclusions of carbon or clay that display a cruciform pattern when viewed in cross-section. A clear variety of andalusite first found in Andalusia, Spain, can be cut into a gemstone. Faceted andalusite stones give a play of red, green, and yellow colors that resemble a muted form of iridescence, although the colors are actually the result of unusually strong pleochroism, an optical phenomenon in which a crystal appears to be different colors when observed at different angles. Andalusite has many industrial uses such as in electrical insulators and as a component in acid-resistant ceramic products. Due to its resemblance to a cross when cut, chiastolite is often worn as an amulet.

Andalusite var. chiastolite crystals showing cruciform patterns in matrix from Austria, small cabinet.
Photo courtesy of Dr. Robert Lavinsky collection.

SYSTEM	Orthorhombic
COLOR	Colorless, white, gray, yellow, pink, reddish-brown, olive green
HARDNESS	7.5
ENVIRONMENT	Metamorphic rocks
OCCURRENCES	Austria, Australia, Brazil, Italy, Spain; California, Maine, Massachusetts, Pennsylvania, USA
VALUE	$20+ per specimen

Metaphysical Properties

Ideal for those with sensitive hearts that often experience feelings of loneliness, depression, and anxiety. This crystal provides a sense of solid ground underneath one's feet to combat against daily stresses and spiritual agitation.

Anglesite

ASTROLOGICAL SIGN

♓

Pisces

VIBRATES TO THE NUMBER

2

RULES

Throat

Third Eye

Crown

Anglesite from Morocco, miniature.
Photo courtesy of Mike Keim collection.

Anglesite is a lead sulfate that forms in translucent to transparent, tabular, thin to thick striated prismatic crystals and is often associated with galena, cerussite, sphalerite, smithsonite, hemimorphite and barite. It has an adamantine luster and does not form as twins, distinguishing it from other similar crystals. Anglesite is primarily collected as a specimen although it can occasionally be cut as a gemstone if sufficiently free of inclusions. Anglesite is named after the Isle of Anglesy, Wales, where it was first discovered.

SYSTEM	Orthorhombic
COLOR	Colorless, white, gray, yellow, green, brown
HARDNESS	2.5-3
ENVIRONMENT	Oxidation zone of lead deposits
OCCURRENCES	Africa, Australia, Germany, Mexico, Spain, Wales; Arizona, Pennsylvania, Utah, Idaho, USA
VALUE	$40+ per specimen

Metaphysical Properties

The crystal that tethers one's guardian angel, or spiritual helper, to the user for the purposes of receiving guidance from those unseen. Useful for those interested in the communication with non-corporeal beings, such as through clairvoyance, as well as assisting in retaining the messages received through dreams after waking up.

Apatite

ASTROLOGICAL SIGN

♊

Gemini

VIBRATES TO THE NUMBER

9

RULES

Third Eye

Blue apatite from Brazil, small cabinet.
Photo courtesy of Dr. Robert Lavinsky collection.

Apatite is a group of minerals containing varying amounts of calcium fluorine-chlorine-hydroxyl phosphate with small amounts of manganese and cerium. Apatite has a greasy, vitreous luster, is transparent to opaque, and forms in hexagonal, prismatic crystals, frequently tabular, and may be short to long in length. Apatite is a common accessory mineral and occurs in many environments. Apatite is widely used in the manufacture of phosphate fertilizers and as salts of phosphoric acid and phosphorus in the chemical industry. Apatite's name comes from the Greek word *apate*, meaning "deceit" due to its tendency to be confused with other minerals such as fluorite or aquamarine. When hard and clear enough, Apatite can be cut and polished as a gemstone.

Apatite crystal from Mexico,
small cabinet. Photo courtesy of
Patti Polk collection.

SYSTEM	Hexagonal
COLOR	Colorless, yellow, green, brown, red, blue
HARDNESS	5
ENVIRONMENT	Metamorphic rocks, iron-rich igneous deposits, pegmatites
OCCURRENCES	Brazil, Canada, Germany, Italy, Mexico, Spain; California, Maine, Massachusetts, USA
VALUE	$10+ per specimen

Metaphysical Properties

Has mentally stimulating properties that may yield lucid dreams when the crystal is placed near the head while sleeping, as well as moments of insight that provides answers to grueling questions one may have.

Apophyllite

ASTROLOGICAL SIGN

♊
Gemini

♎
Libra

VIBRATES TO THE NUMBER

4

RULES

Third Eye

Crown

Apophyllite cluster from India, small cabinet. Photo courtesy of Dr. Robert Lavinsky collection.

Apophyllite is composed of hydrous calcium potassium fluorsilicate and forms as distinct, cubic crystals, often over an inch or two long, with striations on one face and a pearly luster on the cleavage face. Crystals are glassy, and transparent to translucent. Apophyllite is a hydrothermal mineral formed in low temperatures and is often found in basalt cavities in conjunction with prehnite, stibnite, scolecite, and zeolites. Apophyllite clusters make beautiful, showy display specimens and are affordable for most any collector, beginning or experienced.

SYSTEM	Tetragonal
COLOR	Colorless, white, pale pink, pale yellow, green
HARDNESS	4.5-5
ENVIRONMENT	Basaltic cavities, pegmatites, ore veins
OCCURRENCES	Brazil, Germany, India, Italy, Mexico; Michigan, New Jersey, Virginia, USA
VALUE	$10+ per specimen

Metaphysical Properties

Metaphysical Properties: Provides productive objectivity that can assist the user in seeing that the earth and the self are undeniably connected to each other. Gently cleanses away distractions that obstruct the mind from connecting to the spiritual.

Aragonite

ASTROLOGICAL SIGN

Capricorn

VIBRATES TO THE NUMBER

9

"Sputnik" aragonite cluster from Morocco, miniature. Photo courtesy of Dr. Robert Lavinsky collection.

RULES

All Chakras

Aragonite is composed of calcium carbonate and forms as small, elongated, prismatic crystals often twinned, in radiating groups, and also as acicular, columnar or coralloid clusters. Aragonite has a vitreous, resinous luster and is transparent to translucent, often with the qualities of fluorescence and phosphorescence. Aragonite sometimes forms in a radiating cluster known as a "sputnik" or "star" cluster that makes attractive display specimens and is also prized as a healing stone. Aragonite is named for its region of discovery in Aragon Province, Spain.

SYSTEM	Orthorhombic
COLOR	Colorless, white, light yellow, light blue, pale violet, brown
HARDNESS	3.5-4
ENVIRONMENT	Hot-spring deposits, sedimentary formations, ore veins
OCCURRENCES	Austria, China, England, Italy, Mexico, Morocco, Spain; Arizona, Colorado, New Mexico, USA
VALUE	$5+ per specimen

Metaphysical Properties

Aragonite can arouse a productive self-awareness of one's own internal imbalances caused by those long-forgotten emotional traumas that still dictate our lives on a subconscious level. Upon clearing oneself of such emotional obstructions, the user is more likely to further their own spiritual advancement all the while demonstrating love and compassion for others.

Aragonite cluster colored by copper
minerals exhibiting the coralloidal
form from China, cabinet specimen.
Photo courtesy of Travis Hartins collection.

Aurichalcite

ASTROLOGICAL SIGN

Aquarius

RULES

Throat

VIBRATES TO THE NUMBER

2

Third Eye

Aurichalcite with calcite from 79 Mine, Arizona, miniature.
Photo courtesy of Chris Whitney-Smith collection.

Aurichalcite is a basic carbonate of zinc and copper that forms in delicate acicular crystals that produce feathery, tufted crusts or mammillary balls on the surface of the host matrix. Aurichalcite is translucent, has a silky or pearly luster and frequently occurs with limonite, calcite, malachite, and azurite. Aurichalcite is quite soft and delicate so it is mainly of interest to scientists for study and as mineral collector specimens.

SYSTEM	Orthorhombic
COLOR	Green blue to sky blue
HARDNESS	1-2
ENVIRONMENT	Oxidation zone of zinc and copper sulfide deposits
OCCURRENCES	Africa, Greece, France, Mexico, Scotland; Arizona, California, New Mexico, Utah, USA
VALUE	$15+ per specimen

Metaphysical Properties

Alleviates built-up tension and promotes harmony within the user. This crystal stimulates the ability to speak aloud one's emotional desires and needs, thus pulling out poisonous stress from the mind. The overall effect is inner harmony and peace for troubled minds.

Azurite

ASTROLOGICAL SIGN

Sagittarius

VIBRATES TO THE NUMBER

1

RULES

Third Eye

Crown

Azurite sun on kaolinitic sandstone from
Malbunka Copper Mine, Australia, cabinet.
Photo courtesy of Larry Michon collection.

Azurite is a basic copper carbonate that forms as equidimensional or tabular prismatic crystals, often intergrown, in radiating botroyoidal masses, rosettes, and as surface crusts. Azurite is transparent to translucent with a vitreous luster tending towards adamantine. Azurite is a secondary copper mineral and commonly occurs with malachite, limonite, and chalcopryrite in the zone of alteration of hydrothermal replacement deposits and will frequently alter to malachite over time. Azurite and malachite staining on rock surfaces has often proved to be a valuable prospecting guide for the discovery of copper ore deposits and ground azurite has been used as a paint pigment for native people since ancient times. Azurite is primarily a display specimen, but it may occasionally be carved, cut into cabochons or faceted into stones for jewelry making.

Azurite crystal cluster from
Morenci, Arizona, USA, cabinet.
Photo courtesy of Patti Polk collection.

Metaphysical Properties

A student's ideal crystal. Azurite helps to promote retention of information and flexibility of mind. Such flexibility allows for connections between seemingly unrelated materials, thus providing an understanding within the user a sense of harmony. Also stimulates within the user an interest in the selves' role in society.

SYSTEM	Monoclinic
COLOR	Deep azure blue
HARDNESS	3.5-4
ENVIRONMENT	Secondary zone of copper ore deposits
OCCURRENCES	Africa, Australia, Chile, France, Mexico, Romania; Arizona, Utah, USA
VALUE	$15+ per specimen

Barite

ASTROLOGICAL SIGN

Aquarius

RULES

Third Eye

VIBRATES TO THE NUMBER

1

Crown

Barite from France, small cabinet.
Photo courtesy of Mike Keim collection.

Barite is composed of barium sulfate that forms in thin to thick, prismatic, tabular crystals that can grow to be quite large (up to a foot long), and sometimes occurs in groups or plates with fan shaped crystals called "cockscomb" or rosettes called "desert roses." Barite is transparent to translucent, has a vitreous to pearly luster, is heavy for its size, and can be fluorescent in ultraviolet light. Barite is a common gangue mineral that occurs with lead, silver, and antimony sulfides; and with anhydrite, apatite, calcite, fluorite, gypsum and dolomite in a variety of hydrothermal environments. Barite is the main ore of barium and has many industrial uses including the manufacture of glass and paints, in paper and rubber products, and in radiography.

SYSTEM	Orthorhombic
COLOR	Colorless, white, gray, yellow, brown, red, blue
HARDNESS	3-3.5
ENVIRONMENT	Hydrothermal replacement deposits, sedimentary rocks, sulfide ore veins
OCCURRENCES	Africa, England, France, Italy, Morocco; Arizona, Colorado, Connecticut, Oklahoma, Missouri, South Dakota, USA
VALUE	$10+ per specimen

Metaphysical Properties

Barite opens the mind's eye wider to allow higher, spiritual acknowledgment and understanding to descend upon the user. It is also a dream enhancer that can reveal the users own inner, subconscious thoughts in the images and emotions felt in dreams (so keep a dream journal near your bed to see any recurring themes).

Barite crystals from the Magma
Mine, AZ, small cabinet.
Photo courtesy of Chris Whitney-Smith collection.

Benitoite

B

ASTROLOGICAL SIGN

♍

Virgo

RULES

Third Eye

**VIBRATES TO
THE NUMBER**

9

Benitoite with neptunite from San
Benito, California, small cabinet.
Photo courtesy of Mike Keim collection.

Benitoite is barium titanium silicate and forms as short, tabular, prismatic, dipyramidal
crystals, often zoned. Benitoite is transparent to translucent, with a vitreous luster, and
fluoresces under short wave ultraviolet light, appearing bright blue to bluish white in
color. The more rarely seen clear to white benitoite crystals fluoresce red under longwave UV light. Benitoite is a rare mineral and was first described in 1907 by George
D. Louderback, who named it benitoite for its occurrence near the headwaters of the
San Benito River in San Benito County, California.
Benitoite occurs in a limited number of areas, and
gemstone quality material has only been found in
California. In 1985, benitoite was named as the official
state gem of California. Benitoite is highly sought
after as a display specimen and commands high prices.
Deep blue, transparent crystals are cut and faceted as
gemstones.

Metaphysical Properties

Stimulates the psychic
senses that may enhance
both one's ability to
psychically communicate
with one's angelic
guardians as well as
improving the likelihood of
noticing synchronicities.
These synchronicities
pertain to not only
understanding one's
personal life on a deeper
level, but the universe
and its forces as well, like
mathematics and geometry.

SYSTEM	Hexagonal
COLOR	Colorless, shades of blue
HARDNESS	6-6.5
ENVIRONMENT	Hydrothermally altered serpentinite
OCCURRENCES	Japan; Arkansas, California, USA
VALUE	$200+ per specimen

Beryl

Rough beryl crystal from Beauregard Mine,
New Hampshire, USA, cabinet specimen.
Photo courtesy of Larry Michon collection.

Beryl is beryllium aluminum silicate and forms as hexagonal prisms, often without terminations, and prism faces are often finely striated lengthwise. Rarely, beryl will occur as rod-like masses. Beryl is transparent to translucent with a vitreous luster and is often so dense with inclusions that it becomes opaque. Basic beryl is generally fairly opaque, and is grayish-white, yellowish-white or pale blue in color. Transparent, gem-quality beryl occurs in a variety of colors due to different mineral inclusions and is cut and faceted as a precious gemstone. Gem beryl is named according to its color, and includes the varieties aquamarine (blue-green), emerald (green), heliodor (yellow), goshenite (colorless), morganite (pink), and bixbite (red).

SYSTEM	Hexagonal
COLOR	Blue-green, green, yellow, pink, red, colorless, grayish-white, bluish-white
HARDNESS	7.5-8
ENVIRONMENT	Granitic pegmatites, metamorphic rocks
OCCURRENCES	Africa, Brazil, Columbia, India, Italy, Madagascar, Pakistan, Russia; California, Colorado, Connecticut, Georgia, Idaho, Maine, Massachusetts, New Hampshire, New Mexico, North Carolina, South Dakota, Utah, Virginia, USA
VALUE	$40+ per specimen

Metaphysical Properties

This crystal covers an array of enhancing properties because of the variety of colors it may be found in. Aquamarine provides courage; emerald encourages love; heliodor improves one's psychic prowess; goshenite stabilizes emotions; morganite facilitates peaceful encounters; bixbite enhances intuition through insight.

Beryl-Aquamarine

ASTROLOGICAL SIGN

Gemini

Pisces

Aries

**VIBRATES TO
THE NUMBER**

1

RULES

Heart

Throat

Aquamarine crystal from
Pakistan, small cabinet.
Photo courtesy of Kevin Burgart collection.

Beryl-Bixbite

ASTROLOGICAL SIGN

Taurus

Aries

**VIBRATES TO
THE NUMBER**

8

RULES

Root

Heart

Bixbite from Utah, USA, cabinet size.
Photo courtesy of Mike Keim collection.

Beryl-Emerald

ASTROLOGICAL SIGN

Taurus

Gemini

Aries

VIBRATES TO THE NUMBER

4

Emerald on calcite from Columbia, miniature.
Photo courtesy of Mike Keim collection.

RULES

Heart

Beryl-Goshenite

ASTROLOGICAL SIGN

Libra

VIBRATES TO THE NUMBER

3

Goshenite from Pakistan, miniature.
Photo courtesy of Mike Keim collection.

RULES

Third Eye

Crown

Etheric

Beryl-Heliodor

ASTROLOGICAL SIGN

Leo

VIBRATES TO
THE NUMBER

5

RULES

Solar Plexus

Heliodor crystal in quartz matrix from
Connecticut, USA, cabinet specimen.
Photo courtesy of Patti Polk collection.

Beryl-Morganite

ASTROLOGICAL SIGN

Libra

VIBRATES TO
THE NUMBER

3

RULES

Heart

Morganite crystal from Pala, California, USA,
miniature. Photo courtesy of Mike Keim collection.

Biotite

ASTROLOGICAL SIGN

♏

Scorpio

VIBRATES TO
THE NUMBER

8

RULES

Third Eye

Crown

Biotite on orthoclase from Namibia,
Africa, small cabinet. Photo courtesy of
Dr. Robert Lavinsky collection.

Biotite is comprised of hydrous potassium aluminum silicate and is a member of the mica group. Biotite forms rarely in tabular, barrel-shaped, or pseudo-hexagonal crystals and commonly as embedded grains or as plates or sheets. Biotite is flexible, transparent to opaque and has a vitreous to pearly luster. Biotite is a common and important rock-building mineral of many intrusive igneous rocks, pegmatites, and metamorphic rocks. When biotite is found in large chunks, it is called "books" because it resembles a book with many pages. Biotite frequently occurs with muscovite and feldspar and when larger crystals are found in dark volcanic rocks they are known as porphyry phenocrists. Biotite is mainly of interest to specimen collectors as it isn't a mineral that can be cut into gemstones.

SYSTEM	Monoclinic
COLOR	Black, brown, dark green
HARDNESS	2.5-3
ENVIRONMENT	Metamorphic rocks, pegmatites, intrusive igneous rocks, sandstones
OCCURRENCES	Brazil, Canada, Greenland, Italy; Alaska, North Carolina, Virginia, USA
VALUE	$5+ per specimen

Metaphysical Properties

Biotite promotes rationality and objectivity to see situations as being intellectually solvable. Also, this particular, crystal-enhanced insight is coated with feelings of tenderness, meaning that these solutions lack callousness or insensitivity if their outcomes affect others.

Bismuth

ASTROLOGICAL SIGN

Aquarius

VIBRATES TO
THE NUMBER

2

RULES

All
Chakras

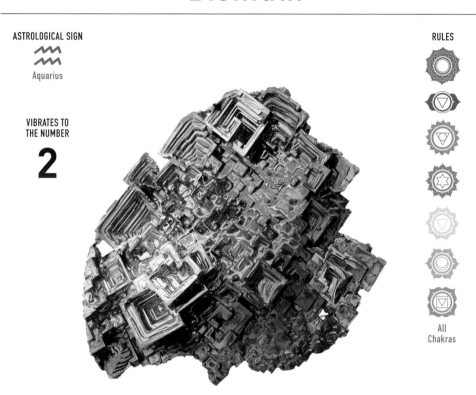

Colorful, iridescent bismuth lab-created by
William Horton. Photo courtesy of William Horton collection.

Bismuth is a native element and occurs rarely as imperfect crystals, but more commonly as lamellar masses and dendritic, branching, or skeletal aggregates. It is often tarnished with an iridescent or brassy coating and is sectile and somewhat malleable when heated. Bismuth may be confused with antimony, but can be recognized by its rose-pink hue. Bismuth is associated with gold, nickel, silver, cobalt and uranium sulfides in hydrothermal veins. Bismuth is the most naturally diamagnetic element, and has one of the lowest values of thermal conductivity among metals. Also as the toxicity of lead has become more apparent in recent years, there is an increasing use of bismuth alloys as a replacement for lead. Beautifully colored bismuth crystals can be lab grown using small pellets of native bismuth. The iridescent color that appears on the surface is due to a thin layer of bismuth oxide that forms on the surface as it cools and the rapid growth creates hollow stepped crystals in the "hopper" habit. Both the natural and man-made crystals are collectible as display pieces.

Bismuth crystals from
Colorado, small cabinet.
Photo courtesy of Patti Polk collection.

SYSTEM	Hexagonal
COLOR	Silver-white, pinkish, metallic
HARDNESS	2-2.5
ENVIRONMENT	Hydrothermal veins, granite pegmatites, hydrothermal replacement deposits
OCCURRENCES	Bolivia, Canada, England, Germany, Madagascar, Norway, Sweden; Colorado, Connecticut, South Carolina, USA
VALUE	$10+ per specimen

Metaphysical Properties

Bismuth relieves feelings of isolation by promoting the connectivity between the user and the spiritual, astral, and physical planes. It also orchestrates a sense of serenity within the user in the face of change and disorder.

Boleite

ASTROLOGICAL SIGN

♉

Taurus

RULES

Third Eye

VIBRATES TO THE NUMBER

5

Boleite crystals on matrix from Amelia Mine, Boleo, Mexico, small cabinet. Photo courtesy of Dr. Robert Lavinsky collection.

Boleite is a rare and complex mineral composed of hydrous lead copper silver chloride hydroxide that forms as pseudocubically twinned crystals, so that each cube-like crystal of boleite is actually composed of three rectangular boxes oriented at right angles to each other. The pseudocubes are sometimes modified by tetragonal dipyramid faces that give the look of octahedral faces. Boleite is translucent, has a vitreous to pearly luster, and is a minor ore of silver, copper, and lead. Boleite was named after its place of discovery, the El Boleo mine, on the Baja Peninsula, near Santa Rosalia, Mexico. Due to its rarity and beauty, boleite is a popular mineral with specimen collectors.

Boleite penetration twin crystal from
Amelia Mine, Mexico, small cabinet.
Photo courtesy of Chris Whitney-Smith collection.

Metaphysical Properties

Through this crystals psychic enhancing properties, the user becomes courageous and productively resilient when confronted with frightening, dangerous, or emotionally traumatic experiences. Stability in an earthly sense is also provided to counteract this psychic prowess, creating harmony within the spiritual and physical aspects of the self.

SYSTEM	Tetragonal
COLOR	Prussian blue to indigo
HARDNESS	3-3.5
ENVIRONMENT	Altered zones of lead and copper deposits
OCCURRENCES	Australia, Chile, England, France, Mexico; Arizona, California, Montana, Nevada, USA
VALUE	$50+ per specimen

Cacoxenite

C

ASTROLOGICAL SIGN

Sagittarius

VIBRATES TO
THE NUMBER

9

Solar Plexus

Crown

Third Eye

RULES

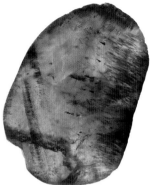

Backlit cut slice of cacoxenite
in amethyst/quartz. Photo courtesy of
Patti Polk collection.

Tiny fans of acicular cacoxenite crystals
on matrix from Ireland, small cabinet.
Photo courtesy of Dr. Robert Lavinsky collection.

Cacoxenite is iron aluminium phosphate and forms as dipyramidal, crudely hexagonal, acicular, crystals; commonly in compact, concentric, spherical to radial aggregates. Cacoxenite is semi-transparent to translucent with a silky luster and is commonly associated with iron ore deposits. Cacoxenite often occurs as an inclusion in quartz that can be cut and faceted as an attractive gemstone for jewelry making. Cacoxenite is often collected as a display specimen and is especially prized as a metaphysical stone when combined with other minerals in quartz crystals known as "Super Seven" crystals.

SYSTEM	Hexagonal
COLOR	Yellow to brownish yellow, reddish orange, golden yellow, deep orange, green
HARDNESS	3-4
ENVIRONMENT	Oxidation zone of magnetic and limonite iron ores, novaculites
OCCURRENCES	Africa, Australia, Brazil, Ireland, Japan, Sweden; Alaska, Georgia, Nevada, New Hampshire, New Jersey, Pennsylvania, Virginia, USA
VALUE	$30+ per specimen

Metaphysical Properties

Cacoxenite cleanses away negativity and promotes communication between the user and the spiritual plane. Cohesively, these aspects allow for the user to register their destiny that such higher powers have planned.

Calcite

RULES

Calcite crystal on pyrite matrix from
Sweetwater Mine, Missouri, USA, cabinet.
Photo courtesy of Larry Michon collection.

All
Chakras

Calcite is composed of calcium carbonate and is one of the most common carbonate minerals found in many environments worldwide. Calcite crystals may be rhombohedral, scalenohedral or prismatic and are often twinned or intergrown. Calcite is transparent to translucent with a vitreous to dull luster and may often be fluorescent. A certain water-clear variety of calcite "Icelandic Spar" exhibits the optical quality of double refraction, or birefringence. Calcite has many uses other than just as a display specimen. It is used in the chemical industry, manufacturing fertilizer, in metallurgy as a flux, and as a component in cement for building construction, besides many others. The many varieties of calcite crystal forms make it a very popular mineral for specimen collectors.

SYSTEM	Hexagonal
COLOR	Colorless, white, yellow, red, green, blue, brown to black, gray
HARDNESS	3
ENVIRONMENT	Sedimentary rocks, metamorphic rocks, hydrothermal veins/replacement deposits
OCCURRENCES	England, Germany, Iceland, Mexico; California, Kansas, Missouri, Oklahoma, New Jersey, New York, Tennessee, USA
VALUE	$5+ per specimen

Metaphysical Properties

All calcites help to clear negative energy and bring an increase in the good vibrations present. Calcite cleanses and promotes a feeling of openness within the user that allows for the joy within the world to be recognized and appreciated. There is a type or color of this crystal that will work at every chakra level.

Single dogtooth calcite
crystal from Elmwood Mine,
Tennessee, USA, cabinet.
Photo courtesy of Larry Michon collection.

Rhombohedral crystal of Iceland Spar calcite exhibiting
bifringence when placed over printed text. From California,
USA, cabinet size. Photo courtesy of Patti Polk collection.

Cavansite

ASTROLOGICAL SIGN

Aquarius

RULES

Third Eye

Crown

VIBRATES TO THE NUMBER

5

Cavansite crystals on matrix
from India, small cabinet.
Photo courtesy of Travis Hartins collection.

Cavansite is composed of hydrous calcium vanadium silicate and generally forms as small radiating prismatic, acicular crystals and as spherulitic rosettes atop a host material. Cavansite has a vitreous to pearly luster and is transparent to translucent. Cavansite is fairly rare and usually occurs as a secondary mineral in basaltic and andesite rocks along with a variety of zeolite minerals. The color of cavansite is distinctive, almost always a vibrant, bright blue and is highly sought after by mineral collectors for its beautiful color and rarity.

Metaphysical Properties

When used during meditation, cavansite can provide the user with psychic abilities to obtain higher knowledge, thus allowing one to acknowledge and understand their inner potential. It is also a stone of truth-telling and peaceful confrontation, allowing the user to speak what is in their heart and mind without tones of crudeness or callousness.

SYSTEM	Orthorhombic
COLOR	Blue
HARDNESS	3-4
ENVIRONMENT	Basalts, andesites, with zeolites
OCCURRENCES	India; Oregon, USA
VALUE	$50+ per specimen

Celestite

ASTROLOGICAL SIGN

Gemini

Capricorn

VIBRATES TO THE NUMBER

8

RULES

Crown

Throat

Single celestite crystal from Colorado, USA, miniature. Photo courtesy of Patti Polk collection.

Celestite is composed of strontium sulfate and forms in thin to thick prismatic or tabular crystals, radiating or parallel, and is transparent to translucent. Celestite has a vitreous to pearly luster, may be fluorescent, and is often associated with halite, gypsum, calcite, galena, and sphalerite. Celestite can sometimes be found lining the internal walls of geodes and one geode found in Ohio weighed close to 300 pounds and contained crystals up to 18 inches across. Celestite contains strontium, a mineral used in the production of fireworks, metal alloys, ceramic glazes, and many other industrial products. Celestite gets its name from the Latin word caelestis, meaning "of the sky" due to its delicate light blue color. Celestite is not generally cut as a gemstone due to its softness and is primarily enjoyed as a collector specimen or healing stone.

Calcite crystals on celestite from the Clay
Center Quarry, Ohio, USA, cabinet specimen.
Photo courtesy of Larry Michon collection.

SYSTEM	Orthorhombic
COLOR	Colorless, white, light blue, pale yellow
HARDNESS	3-3.5
ENVIRONMENT	Evaporate deposits, sedimentary rocks
OCCURRENCES	Canada, Madagascar, Mexico; California, Colorado, Ohio, New York, Texas, USA
VALUE	$10+ per specimen

Metaphysical Properties

A crystal of awareness of realms beyond the physical. With such awareness, communication between the user and their spiritual guides may occur. Thus, this facilitates a sense of having comforting company and alleviates a feeling of spiritual isolation.

C

Cerussite

ASTROLOGICAL SIGN

♍

Virgo

**VIBRATES TO
THE NUMBER**

2

RULES

Root

Crown

Cerussite crystals from Namibia,
Africa, small cabinet. Photo courtesy of
Jeff Scovil, Chris Whitney-Smith collection.

Cerussite is a lead carbonate that forms as elongated crystals that are frequently twinned, with the compound crystals being pseudo-hexagonal in form. Three crystals are usually twinned together on two faces of the prism, producing six-rayed stellate groups with the individual crystals intercrossing at angles of nearly 60 degrees. Cerussite has an admantine to greasy luster, is transparent to translucent, heavy, and can be fluorescent. Associated minerals are galena, barite, smithsonite, and sphalerite. Cerussite is an important ore of lead and it got its name is from the Latin word cerussa, meaning "white lead." Occasionally cerussite can be cut as a gemstone if it has sufficient clarity and hardness.

Metaphysical Properties

Cerussite was historically used by alchemists who hoped to transmutate lead into gold. Now, in modern times, it may also be used to create a positive transmutation within the user. These transformations may then provide alignment with the self and their ambitions, which include, but are not limited to, a career change to better suit their innermost passions.

SYSTEM	Orthorhombic
COLOR	Colorless, white, gray, yellow, brown
HARDNESS	3-3.5
ENVIRONMENT	Oxidation zone of lead deposits
OCCURRENCES	Africa, Australia, Canada, Russia; Arizona, California, Colorado, New Mexico, Pennsylvania, USA
VALUE	$20+ per specimen

Crystal Catalog   69

Chabazite

ASTROLOGICAL SIGN

♍

Virgo

RULES

Crown

VIBRATES TO THE NUMBER

3

Chabazite rhombohedrons on matrix from
Nova Scotia, Canada, cabinet specimen.
Photo courtesy of Dr. Robert Lavinsky collection.

Chabazite is hydrous calcium aluminum silicate and forms as pseudo-cubic, rhombohedral crystals, often as penetration twins. Chabazite is transparent to translucent, has a vitreous luster, and belongs to the zeolite group. Chabazite occurs most commonly in voids and amygdules in basaltic rocks with other zeolites and calcite. Chabazite has no economic or commercial uses and is primarily used as an attractive display specimen by mineral collectors.

SYSTEM	Hexagonal
COLOR	Colorless, white, yellow, orange, pink, greenish or reddish
HARDNESS	4-5
ENVIRONMENT	Cavities in volcanic and intrusive igneous rocks
OCCURRENCES	Bohemia, Canada, Germany, Iceland, India, Italy; Arizona, Oregon, New Jersey, USA
VALUE	$15+ per specimen

Metaphysical Properties

Allows for one to feel comfortable with the self without having the need to have music on to listen to, the television on to keep the eyes busy, etc. A calmness, stillness, and serenity will follow the use of this crystal, which will then bring the user to an acceptance of their emotional and mental struggles, such as with anxiety, old traumas, and addiction.

Chrysoberyl

ASTROLOGICAL SIGN

Leo

**VIBRATES TO
THE NUMBER**

6

Chrysoberyl crystal from Brazil, small cabinet.
Photo courtesy of Mike Keim collection.

RULES

Solar Plexus

Crown

Chrysoberyl is beryllium aluminum oxide and forms as prismatic, tabular crystals, striated, often twinned and forming pseudo-hexagonal crystals. Chrysoberyl is transparent to translucent, has a vitreous to silky luster, and the variety alexandrite exhibits a phenomenon called the "alexandrite effect." The alexandrite variety displays a color change dependent upon the nature of the ambient lighting, changing from greenish to reddish. Because human vision is more sensitive to light in the green spectrum and the red spectrum, alexandrite appears greenish in daylight where a full spectrum of visible light is present and reddish in incandescent light that emits less green and blue spectrum. Another variety of chrysoberyl is a translucent, yellowish, chatoyant chrysoberyl called cymophane or "cat's eye." As a gemstone, alexandrite is generally faceted as a semi-precious stone, and cymophane is cut and polished as a rounded cabochon for setting in jewelry.

SYSTEM	Orthorhombic
COLOR	Colorless, white, yellow, green, greenish-brown, raspberry red
HARDNESS	8.5
ENVIRONMENT	Granite pegmatites
OCCURRENCES	Africa, Brazil, India, Madagascar, Russia, Sri Lanka; Connecticut, Maine, South Dakota, USA
VALUE	$40+ per specimen

Metaphysical Properties

Chrysoberyl can be referred to as the assistant who helps the user strive for progress; progress toward a difficult goal, toward self-improvement, or with strenuous family matters. This is done through an increase of awareness and understanding of the relationships that can be formed with the usage of words, actions, or inactions.

Alexandrite crystal on micaceous
schist from Russia, miniature.
Photo courtesy of Dr. Robert Lavinsky collection.

Chrysocolla

ASTROLOGICAL SIGN

Taurus

Gemini

Virgo

VIBRATES TO THE NUMBER

5

Chrysocolla stalactites with druzy coating from the Ray Mine, Arizona, small cabinet.
Photo courtesy of Chris Whitney-Smith collection.

RULES

Root

Heart

Throat

Chrysocolla is a hydrous copper silicate mineral that forms in the oxidation zone of copper deposits with quartz, limonite, azurite, malachite, cuprite, and other secondary copper minerals. Chrysocolla forms as small stalatitic and botroyoidal masses or crusts, is translucent, and has a vitreous to greasy luster. When in its massive form and strengthened by greater amounts of silica, chrysocolla can be cut, carved, and polished as a decorative stone and cut as beautifully colored cabochons for jewelry making. The name chrysocolla comes from the Greek word chrysos, "gold," and kolla, "glue," in reference to the name of the material used to solder gold in ancient Greece. Chrysocolla is a favorite specimen with mineral collectors due to its beautiful rich blue, aqua, and green colors.

SYSTEM	Monoclinic
COLOR	Blue-green
HARDNESS	2-4
ENVIRONMENT	Oxidation zone of copper deposits
OCCURRENCES	Africa, Chile, Mexico, Russia; Arizona, Idaho, Michigan, New Mexico, Pennsylvania, Utah, USA
VALUE	$20+ per specimen

Metaphysical Properties

Chrysocolla promotes the user to become more attuned with their innate ability to love others and to understand that acts of gentleness are a most profound type of power. The user will find that the ability to express themselves through their words will come much easier and will oftentimes also prove to contain pearls of wisdom.

Cinnabar

VIBRATES TO
THE NUMBER

8

Cinnabar crystals on quartz with
dolomite from China, small cabinet.
Photo courtesy of Dr. Robert Lavinsky collection.

Cinnabar is a sulfide of mercury that forms in rare rhombohedral to thick tabular crystals that are translucent with an adamantine to dull luster. Cinnabar is associated with stibnite, realgar, orpiment, barite, quartz, and opal. Cinnabar is the most common source ore for refining elemental mercury, and is the historic source for the brilliant red or scarlet pigment known as vermilion. The ancient mercury mines at Almaden, Spain, have been in production since the Roman Age, 2000 years ago. Cinnabar has also been used as a cosmetic powder in the Mayan culture, and as the coloring agent for lacquerware since the Song dynasty in China. Because of its mercury content, cinnabar can be toxic to human beings and it is advisable to always wash your hands well if you come in contact with cinnabar or any other toxic minerals. Cinnabar crystals make striking and desirable mineral specimens.

Cinnabar crystals with opalite
from the B & B Mine, Nevada,
USA, cabinet size.
Photo courtesy of Patti Polk.

Metaphysical Properties

Cinnabar contains transformative abilities that can progress the user farther toward their destiny through cleansing away one's own negative thoughts and obsessions over their own imperfections. With such spiritual blockages gone, the results may include a refreshing of one's self-confidence; this may, in turn, lead to new prospects in life, career, or financial stability.

SYSTEM	Hexagonal
COLOR	Bright red, brownish-red
HARDNESS	2-2.5
ENVIRONMENT	Hydrothermal deposits, hot springs, sedimentary rocks
OCCURRENCES	China, Italy, Spain, Yugoslavia; Arkansas, California, Nevada, Oregon, Texas, USA
VALUE	$40+ per specimen

Colemanite

ASTROLOGICAL SIGN

♈

Aries

VIBRATES TO THE NUMBER

7

RULES

Heart

Crown

Colemanite crystal cluster from
Boron, California, small cabinet.
Photo courtesy of Dr. Robert Lavinsky collection.

Colemanite is hydrous calcium borate that forms as short prismatic dipyramidal crystals that are vitreous to dull in luster, transparent to translucent, and sometimes found lining geodes as small druzy crystals. Colemanite is a borate mineral found in evaporate deposits of alkaline lacustrine environments, and is a secondary mineral that forms by alteration of borax and ulexite. Colemanite was first described in 1884 for an occurrence near Furnace Creek in Death Valley and was named after William Tell Coleman (1824–1893), owner of the Harmony Borax Works mine where it was first found. Colemanite is an important ore of boron, and was the most important boron ore until the discovery of kernite in 1926. It has many industrial uses, like the manufacturing of heat resistant glass, a component of rocket fuel, and as an ingredient in strengthening metal alloys.

SYSTEM	Monoclinic
COLOR	Colorless, white, pale gray, pale yellow
HARDNESS	4-4.5
ENVIRONMENT	Evaporate deposits, sedimentary rocks
OCCURRENCES	Argentina, Chile, Turkey; California, Nevada, USA
VALUE	$5+ per specimen

Metaphysical Properties

Used as a healing crystal that can cleanse the whole body of energy blockages and wash away disease. Its effects are powerful enough to clear an agitated mind and to improve bodily performance.

Copper

ASTROLOGICAL SIGN

♉

Taurus

♐

Sagittarius

**VIBRATES TO
THE NUMBER**

1

RULES

Root

Sacral

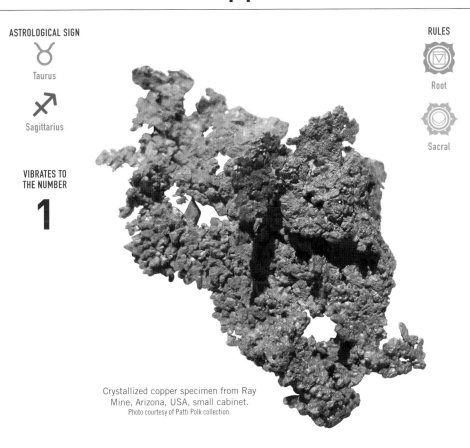

Crystallized copper specimen from Ray
Mine, Arizona, USA, small cabinet.
Photo courtesy of Patti Polk collection.

Copper is a native element and occurs rarely as tetrahexahedral or octahedral crystals that are usually twinned. Copper generally forms in compact masses, plates, or as dendritic branches, and has a metallic luster. Copper is a soft, malleable and ductile metal with high thermal and electrical conductivity. A freshly exposed surface of pure copper has a reddish-orange color, but will patina to a greenish-black color over time as it oxidizes. It is used as a conductor of heat and electricity, as a building material, and as a constituent of various metal alloys. Copper is found as a pure metal in nature, and this was the source of the first metal to be used by humans, ca. 8,000 BC; it was the first metal to be smelted from its ore, ca. 5,000 BC; it was the first metal to be cast into a shape in a mold, ca. 4,000 BC; and it was the first metal to be purposefully alloyed with another metal, tin, to create bronze, ca. 3,500. Today copper has many diverse uses such as in jewelry or decorative art, as a wood preservative, or as an important dietary mineral that helps to build healthy skin, muscle, and bone in the human body.

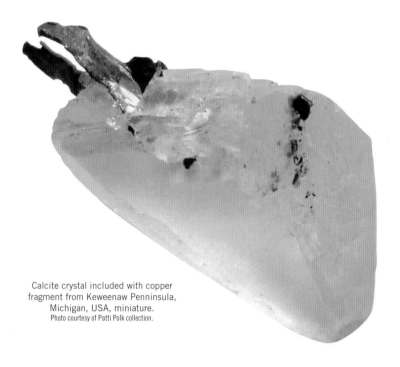

Calcite crystal included with copper
fragment from Keweenaw Penninsula,
Michigan, USA, miniature.
Photo courtesy of Patti Polk collection.

SYSTEM	Isometric
COLOR	Red-orange, brown
HARDNESS	2.5-3
ENVIRONMENT	Oxidation zone of sulfide deposits, hydrothermal replacement deposits, basalts
OCCURRENCES	Africa, Canada, Chile, Germany, Mexico, Sweden; Alaska, Arizona, Michigan, New Jersey, New Mexico, Oregon, USA
VALUE	$10+ per specimen

Metaphysical Properties

Copper's main power is to reduce fatigue and ease restlessness. Both a subduer and an amplifier, it focuses on balancing the physical body without sacrificing vitality or sexuality. Copper is an ideal element that can be helpful in assisting in making rational decisions by reducing physical agitation.

Cordierite

ASTROLOGICAL SIGN

♎
Libra

♐
Sagittarius

♉
Taurus

VIBRATES TO THE NUMBER

7

RULES

Third Eye

Cordierite crystals in matrix from Connecticut, USA, large cabinet. Photo courtesy of Patti Polk collection.

Cordierite is a silicate of aluminum and magnesium that forms as stubby, prismatic crystals, sometimes as pseudo-hexagonal twins, and as granular masses. Cordierite is transparent to translucent and has a vitreous luster. Cordierite is most often recognized as the gemstone *iolite* and is well known for its property of pleochroism, the appearance of changing color when viewed from different angles. The Vikings knew of this property and used the stone for navigation, as the stone could indicate the direction of the sun on overcast days, hence its name "Viking compass." Gem quality cordierite (iolite) is also known by the name water sapphire and is cut and faceted into beautiful gemstones for jewelry making.

Cordierite crystals on matrix from New Hampshire, USA, large cabinet. Photo courtesy of Dr. Robert Lavinsky collection.

SYSTEM	Orthorhombic
COLOR	Blue or violet when viewed parallel to the prism base, colorless or gray when viewed vertically
HARDNESS	7-7.5
ENVIRONMENT	Contact metamorphic rocks, granitic plutonic rocks
OCCURRENCES	Bavaria, Brazil, Canada, Finland, Norway, Madagascar, Sri Lanka; Connecticut, New Hampshire, USA
VALUE	$25+ per specimen

Metaphysical Properties

Cordierite assists in the ability to travel to higher planes, thus allowing the user to become attuned to the higher knowledge that dictates one's responsibility of striving for excellence through endurance. It is also a harmonizer that promotes the connectedness between opposites, such as the masculine and feminine characteristics within everyone.

Corundum

ASTROLOGICAL SIGN

Sagittarius

VIBRATES TO THE NUMBER

1

Corundum is aluminum oxide that forms in prismatic, six-sided crystals with tapered bipyramidal terminations that typically contain traces of iron, titanium, vanadium and chromium. Corundum can vary from opaque to transparent, and the transparent varieties are cut and faceted as precious gemstones. Corundum has a vitreous to adamantine luster, and is extremely hard, second only to diamond on the Mohs scale. Red corundum is called ruby and all other gem-quality corundum is called sapphire, which occurs in a variety of colors depending on the included mineral impurities. Some rubies and sapphires have a "star" or "cats-eye" effect due to crystallographically oriented inclusions of rutile, and corundum may often be fluorescent. Top-quality faceted rubies and sapphires are rare gemstones and command high prices. Low-grade corundum is frequently used as an abrasive in the manufacturing industry. Corundum is commonly synthesized in the lab today in a form known as a "boule" that is often cut as gemstones for jewelry making, and buyers need to be aware when they are purchasing a gemstone if it is natural or a synthetic one, especially if they are paying a high price.

Ruby

Additional Properties: Ruby is a noble protector that will ward off psychic attacks, bad dreams, and unhappiness. Ruby also encourages the user to follow their passions as opposed to staying within a bad place in life that only offers dark corners.

Sapphire

Additional Properties: Sapphire brings beauty and joy to mind when combating against unwanted, negative thoughts. The user will experience a sense of prosperity and fulfillment in life when these desires are consciously bestowed upon the crystal.

SYSTEM	Trigonal
COLOR	Ruby: Red; Sapphire: Blue, pink, pink-orange (padparadscha), yellow, green, violet, colorless
HARDNESS	9
ENVIRONMENT	Metamorphic rocks, pegmatites, plutonic rocks
OCCURRENCES	Afghanistan, Burma, Cambodia, India, Sri Lanka, Thailand; Montana, North Carolina, USA
VALUE	$110+ per carat for a single, cabochon grade ruby crystal

Metaphysical Properties

Corundum promotes intuition that can assist in dealing with and finding solutions for new and challenging issues. It is a crystal of resilience, courage, and perseverance that encourages positive thoughts and banishes negative ones.

Corundum-Ruby

ASTROLOGICAL SIGN

Cancer

Leo

Scorpio

RULES

Root

Heart

VIBRATES TO
THE NUMBER

3

Ruby crystals from Cambodia, thumbnail.
Photo courtesy of Dr. Robert Lavinsky collection.

Corundum-Sapphire

ASTROLOGICAL SIGN

Virgo

Gemini

Libra

Sapphire crystals
on micaeous schist
from Afghanistan,
small cabinet.
Photo courtesy of Dr. Robert
Lavinsky collection.

RULES

Third Eye

Throat

VIBRATES TO
THE NUMBER

2

Star sapphire polished
cabochon from Sri Lanka.
Photo courtesy of Patti Polk collection.

Covellite

ASTROLOGICAL SIGN

Sagittarius

**VIBRATES TO
THE NUMBER(S)**

4 & 7

Covellite crystals on matrix from
Montana, USA, cabinet.
Photo courtesy of Patti Polk collection.

RULES

All
Chakras

Covellite is a rare copper sulfide mineral that forms as thin, platy hexagonal crystals and rosettes that is commonly found with, and as coatings on, chalcocite, chalcopyrite, bornite, enargite, pyrite, and other sulfides. Covellite has a submetallic to dull luster, is heavy, and has a strong blue iridescence. Covellite is found in limited abundance and is not an important ore of copper itself, although it is well known to mineral collectors. Covellite is associated with chalcocite in zones of secondary enrichment of copper sulfide deposits and it often occurs as pseudomorphic replacements after other minerals.

SYSTEM	Hexagonal
COLOR	Iridescent blue, indigo
ENVIRONMENT	Altered hydrothermal copper veins, hydrothermal metamorphic rocks
OCCURRENCES	Bolivia, Chile, Italy, Sardinia; Alaska, Colorado, Montana, Utah, USA
VALUE	$25+ per specimen

Metaphysical Properties

Through covellite's psychic enhancing abilities, the user may experience an increase in periods of calm, reflective reasoning that can lead to recognizing the common mistakes one makes in daily life. Then, through this recognition, one may find opportunity for correction. Because of the radical possibilities presented for change, the user may experience successive small alterations that will eventually prove to become one large, necessary change.

Creedite

ASTROLOGICAL SIGN

Virgo

VIBRATES TO THE NUMBER

6

RULES

Third Eye

Crown

Transpersonal/ Etheric

Creedite crystals with green fluorite crystal from Mexico, cabinet specimen.
Photo courtesy of Trinas Rock Shop.

Creedite is a calcium aluminium sulfate fluoro hydroxide mineral that forms as prismatic crystals that may be bladed, and as acicular radiating sprays or aggregates of fine prisms. It is translucent to transparent and has a vitreous to greasy luster. Creedite was named after the location where it was discovered in 1916 in the Colorado Fluorspar Co. Mine, Mineral County, Colorado. Creedite typically occurs with low-grade metamorphic rocks on a fluorite – calcite – quartz matrix or on a sulfide-matrix and may be associated with fluorite, kaolinite, limonite, kaolinite, smithsonite, and hemimorphite.

SYSTEM	Monoclinic
COLOR	Colorless, white. orange, violet
HARDNESS	3.5-4
ENVIRONMENT	Oxidation zone of fluorite deposits, metamorphic rocks
OCCURRENCES	Bolivia, China, Kazakhstan, Mexico; Arizona, California, Colorado, Nevada, USA
VALUE	$20+ per specimen

Metaphysical Properties

Creedite is a spiritual translator and helper when communicating with the spiritual realms, such as in tarot readings, contacting guardian angels, or calling on spirit guides. Creedite may also provide access to the user's forgotten memories that may be useful in the present.

Crocoite

C

ASTROLOGICAL SIGN

♈

Aries

RULES

Root

VIBRATES TO THE NUMBER

7

Heart

Crown

Crocoite crystals on matrix from the Red Lead Mine, Tasmania, Australia, thumbnail.
Photo courtesy of Dr. Robert Lavinsky collection.

Crocoite is a rare secondary mineral consisting of lead chromate. Crocoite is commonly found as large, well-developed prismatic crystals, sometimes striated or hollow, in acicular groups. Crystals are translucent, and have an adamantine to vitreous luster. Crocoite is frequently associated with wulfenite, cerussite, and vanadinite, and crystals are eagerly sought after by collectors due to their rarity and bright red-orange color. As crocoite is composed of lead chromate it is toxic, containing both lead and hexavalent chromium and exposure to UV light can cause it to lose some of its brilliancy and translucency. The element chromium was first extracted from crocoite.

SYSTEM	Monoclinic
COLOR	Orange, red, yellow
HARDNESS	2.5-3
ENVIRONMENT	Hydrothermal replacement deposits
OCCURRENCES	Brazil, Philippines, Russia, Tasmania; Arizona, California, Pennsylvania, USA
VALUE	$100+ per specimen

Metaphysical Properties

Through the attuning of the spiritual self to this crystal, the user may experience an increase in spiritual awareness that can provide a healing of the human heart. Crocoite also encourages passion and boldness while enhancing creative prowess.

C

Cuprite

ASTROLOGICAL SIGN

♍
Virgo

♑
Capricorn

♉
Taurus

VIBRATES TO THE NUMBER

2

RULES

Root

Sexual/
Creative

Cuprite crystals on matrix from the
Republic of Congo, Africa, miniature.
Photo courtesy of Chris Whitney-Smith collection.

Cuprite is a copper oxide and an important secondary ore of copper. Cuprite forms as octahedral, dodecahedral, or cubic crystals, and as hair-like coatings on native copper crystals or lining cavities in limonite, and penetration twins can often occur. Cuprite is submetallic, translucent to semi-opaque, with an adamantine luster. Minerals associated with cuprite are native copper, malachite, azurite, calcite, and limonite. The name cuprite comes from the Latin word cuprum, meaning "copper." A variety of cuprite crystals that sometimes form on the surface of some limonites is so densely packed that is it called "plush copper" due to its resemblance to velvet. Cuprite mineral specimens are beautiful and a popular mineral with specimen collectors. Although a soft stone, occasionally a transparent cuprite has been cut as a gemstone and they are rare and quite beautiful.

SYSTEM	Isometric
COLOR	Ruby red, dark red
HARDNESS	3.5-4
ENVIRONMENT	Oxidation zone of copper deposits
OCCURRENCES	Africa, Australia, Bolivia, Chile, England, France; Arizona, New Mexico, Utah, USA
VALUE	$20+ per specimen

Metaphysical Properties

Cuprite encourages the feminine polarity within the user in a creative, productive, and powerful way. This feminine-attributed crystal is ideal for those who wish to connect with others but often find that connection is daunting, intimidating, or difficult to do because of prior relationships that were poorly nurtured.

Danburite

ASTROLOGICAL SIGN

♌
Leo

VIBRATES TO THE NUMBER

4

RULES

Heart

Crown

Danburite cluster, Mexico, small cabinet.
Photo courtesy of Patti Polk; Dick Moore collection.

Danburite is a calcium borosilicate mineral that forms as striated, prismatic crystals that are transparent to translucent with a vitreous luster. Danburite is associated with quartz, cassiterite, fluorite, and orthoclase and is sometimes mistaken for topaz. Danburite is named for its first known location in Danbury, Connecticut, and its clarity, brilliance, and hardness often make it valuable as a cut and faceted gemstone for jewelry.

SYSTEM	Orthorhombic
COLOR	Colorless, white, gray, pale pink, pale yellow
HARDNESS	7
ENVIRONMENT	Contact metamorphic rocks
OCCURRENCES	Brazil, Japan, Mexico, Switzerland; Connecticut, New York, USA
VALUE	$20+ per specimen

Metaphysical Properties

Danburite facilitates a relationship with the user's spiritual guardians in a way that allows the user to feel comfort rather than intimidation from higher powers. With such freeing abilities, one may then experience a decrease in daily anxiety, fear, or apprehension toward change.

Single danburite crystal,
Mexico, miniature.
Photo courtesy of Patti Polk collection.

Datolite

Aries

VIBRATES TO THE NUMBER

5

Solar Plexus

Heart

Third Eye

Crown

Transpersonal/ Etheric

Datolite crystal cluster from Cloverdale, California, USA, miniature.
Photo courtesy of Mike Keim collection.

Datolite is a basic calcium borosilicate that occurs as short, prismatic to blunt wedge-shaped complex crystals, and also as fine-grained porcelain-like nodular masses. Datolite is transparent to translucent with a vitreous luster and is associated with zeolites, prehnite, and calcite in cavities in basalts and serpentines. The porcelain variety of datolite colored by copper from the Keweenaw Peninsula, Michigan, is highly collectible as a mineral specimen in its own right and may be cut as cabochons for jewelry making. Water-clear datolite crystals may also occasionally be cut as cabochons or faceted as gemstones.

SYSTEM	Monoclinic
COLOR	Colorless, white, pale green, pale yellow, pale gray
HARDNESS	5-5.5
ENVIRONMENT	Basalts, serpentines, hydrothermal deposits
OCCURRENCES	Canada, Germany, Italy, Mexico, Tasmania; California, Massachusetts, Michigan, New Jersey, USA
VALUE	$20+ per specimen

Metaphysical Properties

During emotionally trying or frustrating situations, datolite may provide rationality and objectivity to allow the user to make clear-headed decisions. The heart may then be cleansed with a calmness that can only be obtained from communicating one's feelings through a strong mind as opposed to an agitated heart.

Diamond

ASTROLOGICAL SIGN

♈
Aries

♌
Leo

♉
Taurus

VIBRATES TO THE NUMBER

33

RULES

Heart

Third Eye

Crown

A 14.87 ct. rough diamond crystal from Eastern-Siberian Region, Russia.
Photo courtesy of Joe Budd; Dr. Robert Lavinsky collection.

Diamond is a native element composed of carbon that usually forms as octahedral, rounded crystals that are transparent to translucent with an adamantine luster. Diamond is the hardest mineral on the Mohs scale and some stones may be fluorescent. Most natural diamonds are formed at high temperature and pressure at depths of 140 to 190 kilometers within the Earth and the growth occurs over periods from 1 billion to 3.3 billion years. Diamonds were brought close to the Earth's surface through deep volcanic eruptions of magma, which cooled into igneous rocks known as kimberlites and lamproites. Diamonds can also be produced synthetically by methods that simulate the conditions of diamond formation in the Earth's mantle. Diamonds have been collected and used by mankind since ancient times as beautiful gemstones and also have many other uses today, such as high-quality abrasives in the manufacturing industry.

SYSTEM	Isometric
COLOR	Colorless, yellow, pink, green, blue, brown, black
HARDNESS	10
ENVIRONMENT	Plutonic rocks (kimberlite breccias), sedimentary placer deposits
OCCURRENCES	Africa, Brazil, Canada, India, Russia; Arkansas, California, USA
VALUE	$50+ per carat, rough low grade specimen

Metaphysical Properties

Diamond is a crystal of endurance, resilience, and intensity that can provide the same for the user. In addition to these, the user's human heart is affected most positively with feelings of courage and the desire to release unnecessary, negative emotions.

Dioptase

ASTROLOGICAL SIGN

Sagittarius

Scorpio

VIBRATES TO THE NUMBER

8

RULES

Heart

Dioptase crystals on calcite from Namibia, Africa, miniature.
Photo courtesy of Dr. Robert Lavinsky collection.

Dioptase is a basic copper silicate that forms as stubby prismatic crystals with rhombohedral terminations, is transparent to translucent and has a vitreous luster. Dioptase is an uncommon mineral found mostly in desert regions where it forms as a secondary mineral in the oxidized zone of copper sulfide mineral deposits. Dioptase commonly occurs with limonite, chrysocolla, and malachite. Ground dioptase was used as a pigment to paint the edges of the eyes on Pre-Pottery Neolithic lime plaster statues discovered at Ain Ghazal, Jordan, that date back to circa 7200 BC. Dioptase is highly valued as a collector specimen and often faceted as a gemstone, if it is transparent enough.

SYSTEM	Hexagonal
COLOR	Emerald green, bluish-green
HARDNESS	5
ENVIRONMENT	Oxidation zone of copper deposits, hydrothermal replacement deposits
OCCURRENCES	Africa, Chile, Mexico, Russia; Arizona, USA
VALUE	$40+ per specimen

Metaphysical Properties

Dioptase is a facilitator and encourager of forgiveness—both of the self and of others. Through forgiveness, you will experience life differently, more potently, because there will be nothing tethering you to a past that hinders your present or your future.

Dolomite

ASTROLOGICAL SIGN

Aries

VIBRATES TO
THE NUMBER

3

Dolomite crystal cluster, Mexico, small cabinet.
Photo courtesy of Patti Polk, Dick Moore collection.

Dolomite with cinnabar crystals from China, small cabinet.
Photo courtesy of Mike Keim collection.

RULES

All
Chakras

Dolomite is calcium magnesium carbonate and generally forms as rhombohedral crystals, often with curved faces or saddle-shaped, and is transparent to translucent with a vitreous to pearly luster. Dolomite occurs with galena, sphalerite, and calcite in low-temperature veins and is found in many locations, but well-formed crystals are not overly abundant. Dolomite is used as an ornamental stone, a concrete aggregate, and in the production of magnesium. It is an important petroleum reservoir rock, and serves as the host rock for large strata-bound Mississippi Valley-type ore deposits of base metals such as lead, zinc, and copper. Where calcite limestone is uncommon or too costly, dolomite is sometimes used in its place as a flux for the smelting of iron and steel. Dolomite may be fluorescent under UV light.

SYSTEM	Hexagonal
COLOR	Colorless, white, pink, gray, green, brown
HARDNESS	3.5-4
ENVIRONMENT	Carbonate sedimentary rocks, metamorphic rocks, hydrothermal veins
OCCURRENCES	Canada, China, England, Italy, Mexico, Spain, Switzerland; California, Colorado, Missouri, North Carolina, USA
VALUE	$10+ per specimen

Metaphysical Properties

A grounding mineral that encourages feelings of acceptance of the self, including flaws, disabilities, and things that cannot be changed. Through such harsh understanding, the user can then experience life with less dissatisfaction and more appreciation for the small things, the precious things. There is goodness everywhere, but obsessing over unchangeable aspects will only prevent that goodness from being recognized.

Enargite

ASTROLOGICAL SIGN

♓

Pisces

VIBRATES TO THE NUMBER

7

RULES

Solar Plexus

Heart

Enargite crystals on matrix from the Butte, Montana, USA, thumbnail.
Photo courtesy of Mike Keim collection.

Enargite is copper arsenic sulfide and forms as prismatic, tabular, or elongated crystals, with vertical striations and as lamellar aggregates or granular masses. Enargite is opaque with a metallic luster and is a fairly important ore of copper and arsenic. Enargite is associated with galena, pyrite, bornite, and covellite. Enargite is used primarily as a display specimen and not cut or polished for jewelry making.

SYSTEM	Orthorhombic
COLOR	Steel gray, gray-black, iron-black
HARDNESS	3
ENVIRONMENT	Mesothermal ore veins, hydrothermal replacement deposits
OCCURRENCES	Africa, Chile, Japan, Mexico, Peru; Alaska, California, Montana, Utah, USA
VALUE	$10+ per specimen

Metaphysical Properties

A mineral of logic and analysis; ideal for the student in everyone. The human heart's desire for making connections with objects, ideas, and people is put to rational use through this crystal's ability to marry insight and our natural problem-solving abilities.

Epidote

ASTROLOGICAL SIGN

Gemini

**VIBRATES TO
THE NUMBER**

2

Quartz crystal with epidote
crystal inclusions from
Pakistan, thumbnail.
Photo courtesy of Mike Keim collection.

RULES

All
Chakras

Epidote is a calcium aluminum iron silicate that forms as prismatic, columnar crystals, often with finely striated faces, also as thick tabular crystals and radiating or wheat-sheaf aggregates. Epidote is transparent to translucent with a vitreous luster. Epidote is a fairly common constituent of rocks and is found in many locations worldwide. Minerals associated with epidote are albite, calcite, zeolites, chlorite, hornblende and actinolite. The name epidote is also used to reference a group of related minerals with complex structures that include epidote, zoisite, clinozoisite, piemontite, and allanite. Epidote is generally admired as a display specimen, but can also be cut and faceted as a gemstone.

SYSTEM	Monoclinic
COLOR	Shades of green with yellow, gray or black tints
HARDNESS	6-7
ENVIRONMENT	Metamorphic rocks, pegmatites, altered igneous rocks
OCCURRENCES	Austria, Brazil, France, Italy, Mexico, Norway, Russia; Alaska, Arizona, California, Connecticut, Massachusetts, North Carolina, USA
VALUE	$20+ per specimen

Metaphysical Properties

A crystal of courage that assists the user in doing things that would normally be too intimidating or frightening to do otherwise. It may also enhance the human heart's natural healing abilities so that the past may not seem so frightening (and the user may not think so negatively about it) now that the present is occurring.

Bow-tie or wheat sheaf-shaped
epidote crystals on matrix from
Mexico, small cabinet.
Photo courtesy of Patti Polk collection.

Erythrite

ASTROLOGICAL SIGN

♍

Virgo

♑

Capricorn

♉

Taurus

VIBRATES TO THE NUMBER

2

RULES

Root

Erythrite crystals on matrix from Bou Azer, Morocco, cabinet.
Photo courtesy of Dr. Robert Lavinsky collection.

Erythrite is hydrous cobalt arsenate and mainly occurs as a secondary coating known as *cobalt bloom* on cobalt arsenide minerals. Well-formed crystals are rare, but do occur as small acicular, prismatic, striated crystals in radiating aggregates with most of the mineral manifesting in crusts or small reniform druzy surfaces. Erythrite is transparent to translucent and has a vitreous or pearly luster and forms as a secondary mineral by the alteration of arsenides and sulfides of cobalt, making it a reliable indicator of cobalt mineral deposits. Due to its softness erythrite is only used as a display specimen.

SYSTEM	Monoclinic
COLOR	Bluish-pink to deep raspberry or purple-red
HARDNESS	1.5-2.5
ENVIRONMENT	Oxidation zone of cobalt-bearing mesothermal veins, contact metamorphic rocks
OCCURRENCES	Australia, Canada, England, France, Germany, Iran, Italy, Mexico, Morocco; California, Idaho, Nevada, USA
VALUE	$15+ per specimen

Metaphysical Properties

Erythrite facilitates communication between the user and others, which can then stimulate the beginnings of long lasting harmony between all parties involved. With such openness of communication between various people(s), further possibilities in life, relationships, and career may also open up.

Feldspar Group

ASTROLOGICAL SIGN

Aquarius

VIBRATES TO THE NUMBER

9

The feldspar group is series of tectosilicates that have varying amounts of the minerals aluminum, calcium, potassium, and sodium between them. Feldspar crystals are generally prismatic, columnar or tabular, frequently twinned, and can grow to be large; also bladed, massive and as aggregates. Feldspar is transparent to opaque, has a vitreous to resinous or pearly luster, and some varieties exhibit optical phenomena. The two main groups we are concerned with here are the *alkali feldspars* and the *plagioclase feldspars*. The alkali feldspars contain the members *orthoclase*, *sanidine*, *microcline*, and *anorthoclase*. The plagioclase feldspars contain the members *albite*, *oligoclase*, *andesine*, *labradorite*, *bytownite*, and *anorthite*. Almost all of the feldspar crystals are quite collectible as mineral specimens and some are cut as gemstones or as decorative stones. The blue-green variety of microcline, known as *amazonite*, is a desirable semiprecious stone that makes for sensational display specimens, especially in combination with smoky quartz, and is also cut as cabochons or beads for jewelry making. The adularescent (bluish iridescence) variety of orthoclase called *moonstone* is also cut as a gemstone, as is *sunstone*, an oligoclase feldspar member that exhibits the shimmering "schiller" effect, caused by tiny inclusions of copper flakes. Labradorite is well known for its beautiful iridescent play of colors and it too is cut as a gemstone for jewelry making and polished as an ornamental piece.

SYSTEM	Triclinic or monoclinic
COLOR	Colorless, white, gray, yellow, pink, blue, blue-green, reddish, brown
HARDNESS	6-6.5
ENVIRONMENT	Granitic pegmatites, metamorphic rocks, plutonic and volcanic igneous rocks
OCCURRENCES	Brazil, Madagascar, Norway, Soviet Union, India, Namibia; Colorado, Oregon, Virginia, USA
VALUE	$20+ per specimen

Metaphysical Properties

The feldspar group, as a whole, provides the user with both internal and externally received messages that have been otherwise forgotten, misplaced, or no longer thought to have been in reach. A supporter of the unconventional and innovative thought process that may provide exciting new methods for doing things.

Feldspar-Albite

ASTROLOGICAL SIGN

Aquarius

VIBRATES TO
THE NUMBER

22

RULES

Third Eye

Crown

Plagioclase feldspar var. albite crystals on matrix
from Colorado, USA, cabinet specimen.
Photo courtesy of Patti Polk; Dick Moore collection.

Feldspar-Amazonite

ASTROLOGICAL SIGN

Virgo

VIBRATES TO
THE NUMBER

5

RULES

Heart

Throat

Microcline feldspar var. amazonite crystals
from Colorado, USA, small cabinet.
Photo courtesy of Patti Polk collection.

Feldspar-Labradorite

ASTROLOGICAL SIGN

Sagittarius

♏
Scorpio

♌
Leo

**VIBRATES TO
THE NUMBER(S)**

6 & 7

Plagioclase feldspar var.
labradorite specimen from
Madagascar, large cabinet.
Photo courtesy of Patti Polk collection.

RULES

All
Chakras

Feldspar-Moonstone

ASTROLOGICAL SIGN

♋
Cancer

♎
Libra

♏
Scorpio

**VIBRATES TO
THE NUMBER**

4

Orthoclase feldspar var. moonstone crystals on
matrix from Chihuahua, Mexico, small cabinet.
Photo courtesy of Dr. Robert Lavinsky collection.

RULES

Third Eye

Crown

F

Feldspar-Oligoclase

Light blue, gemmy
oligoclase feldspar
specimen from Spruce
Pine, NC. Cabinet size.
Photo courtesy of Dr. Robert
Lavinsky collection.

Feldspar-Orthoclase

Faceted yellow feldspar var. orthoclase
crystal from Madagascar, micromount.
Photo courtesy of Patti Polk; Lamont Latham collection.

Feldspar-Sunstone

Oligoclase feldspar var. sunstone crystal
from Tanzania, Africa, thumbnail.
Photo courtesy of Kevin Burgart collection.

Fluorite

ASTROLOGICAL SIGN

♓
Pisces

♑
Capricorn

**VIBRATES TO
THE NUMBER**

7

Purple zoned octahedron fluorite cube from
Cave-in-Rock, Illinois, USA, thumbnail.
Photo courtesy of Patti Polk collection.

RULES

All
Chakras

Fluorite is calcium fluoride and commonly forms as cubes, octahedrons, and dodecahedrons; and occasionally as penetration twins. Fluorite is transparent to translucent, has a vitreous luster and fluoresces under UV light, usually blue or violet. Fluorite is a widely occurring mineral that occurs globally with significant deposits in over 9,000 areas. It may occur as a vein deposit, especially with metallic minerals, where it often forms a part of the gangue (the surrounding "host-rock" in which valuable minerals occur) and may be associated with galena, sphalerite, barite, quartz, and calcite. It is a common mineral in deposits of hydrothermal origin and has been noted as a primary mineral in granites and other igneous rocks and as a common minor constituent of limestone. Fluorite is allochromatic, meaning that it can be tinted with elemental impurities. Fluorite comes in a wide range of colors and has consequently been dubbed "the most colorful mineral in the world." Every color of the rainbow in various shades is represented by fluorite samples, along with black and colorless crystals. The most common colors are purple, blue, green, or yellow. Less common are pink, red, brown, colorless, and black. Color zoning or banding is commonly present. The color of the fluorite is determined by factors including impurities, exposure to radiation, and the absence or voids of the color centers. Natural fluorite has many lapidary uses, such as in drilled beads for use in jewelry making, and carved for ornamental decorative pieces.

Yellow fluorite with a purple
phantom, Cave-in-Rock,
Illinois, USA, small cabinet.
Photo courtesy of Mike Keim collection.

Green fluorite on calcite
and sphalerite matrix from
the Nikolai Mine, Siberia,
Russia, small cabinet.
Photo courtesy of Dr. Robert Lavinsky
collection.

Metaphysical Properties

Fluorite provides realigning of one's emotions and thoughts from disorderly to orderly, especially through meditation. Fluorite increases the ability to concentrate, balances the mind, and be more discerning in recognizing the truth behind illusion. Fluorite also provides stabilizing energy for purifying, cleansing, and nourishing the body.

SYSTEM	Isometric
COLOR	Colorless, yellow, green, blue, pink, purple, red, brown, black
HARDNESS	4
ENVIRONMENT	Hydrothermal veins, metamorphic rocks, volcanic rocks
OCCURRENCES	Brazil, Canada, China, England, Italy, Mexico, Switzerland; Colorado, Illinois, Kentucky, Ohio, USA
VALUE	$30+ per specimen

Rare pink fluorite with crown of colorless
fluorite on top, Mongolia, thumbnail.
Photo courtesy of Larry Michon collection.

Blue fluorite crystal from Bingham,
New Mexico, USA, thumbnail.
Photo courtesy of Kevin Burgart collection.

Galena

ASTROLOGICAL SIGN

♑

Capricorn

RULES

Root

VIBRATES TO
THE NUMBER

22

Galena cubes on matrix with calcite, Sweetwater Mine, Missouri, USA, thumbnail. Photo courtesy of Larry Michon collection.

Galena is lead sulfide and commonly occurs as cubes and octahedrons in singular cubes or compact masses, occasionally as dodecahedrons, is heavy, and opaque with a silvery metallic luster. Galena, also known as *lead glance*, is the most important ore of lead and an important source of silver. Galena is one of the most abundant and widely distributed sulfide minerals and often associated with the minerals sphalerite, calcite, and fluorite.

One of the oldest uses of galena was as kohl, which in ancient Egypt, was applied around the eyes to reduce the glare of the desert sun and to repel flies. Today, galena is mainly collected as an interesting display specimen and is not cut for any type of jewelry-making purposes or for use in personal products due to its toxicity.

Metaphysical Properties

All colors of this crystal allow for the user's creative aspirations and goals to become realities in the physical realm without provoking the user to commit irrational or threatening acts to manifest these realities. This crystal also spurs feelings of commitment and devotion within the user, both of which are necessary for one's ability to manifest their dreams into this world.

SYSTEM	Isometric
COLOR	Lead-gray
HARDNESS	2.5
ENVIRONMENT	Hydrothermal replacement deposits, metamorphic rocks
OCCURRENCES	China, France, Germany, Italy, Spain, Yugoslavia; California, Colorado, Idaho, Kansas, Missouri, Oklahoma, USA
VALUE	$5+ per specimen

Garnet Group

Leo

Virgo

Capricorn

Aquarius

**VIBRATES TO
THE NUMBER**

2

All
Chakras

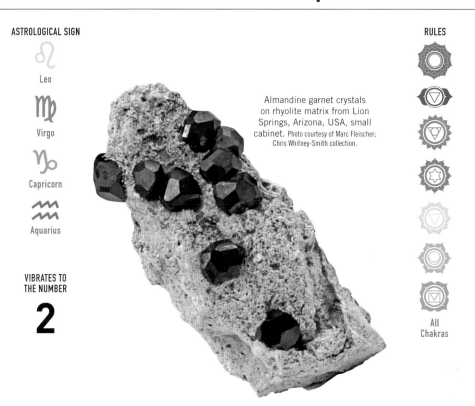

Almandine garnet crystals
on rhyolite matrix from Lion
Springs, Arizona, USA, small
cabinet. Photo courtesy of Marc Fleischer;
Chris Whitney-Smith collection.

The garnet group is a group of closely related aluminum silicates that include *pyrope*, *almandine*, and *spessartine*, and calcium silicates *grossular*, *andradite*, and *uvarovite* that are determined by the varying amounts of included magnesium, iron, and manganese. Garnets commonly form as dodecahedral or trapezohedral crystals, and also as rounded grains and compact masses. Garnets are transparent to opaque, have a resinous to vitreous luster, and many fluoresce under UV light. The varieties are:

Pyrope: Magnesium aluminum silicate. Colors: Blood-red, purplish-red (var. rhodolite).

Almandine: Iron aluminum silicate. Colors: Red with violet or brown tints.

Spessartine: Manganese aluminum silicate. Colors: Orange-yellow, orange-red or pink, brownish yellow.

Grossular: Calcium aluminum silicate. Colors: Colorless, pink, yellow, red, green (var. tsavorite), brownish-orange yellow (var. hessonite).

Andradite: Calcium iron silicate. Colors: Brownish-red, yellow, yellow-green or yellow-brown, green (var. demantoid), black.

Uvarovite: Calcium chromium silicate. Colors: Green.

Some garnets may exhibit an unusual visual effect called *asterism* (the rayed-star effect). Asterism is usually associated with star sapphire and star ruby, but there are a number of other gemstones that can occasionally exhibit this effect. The other gemstones that can exhibit asterism include moonstone, quartz, spinel, citrine, diopside, emerald, chrysoberyl, and beryl. The garnet varieties that may exhibit asterism are almandine and a mixture of almandine and pyrope garnet. Star garnets are usually opaque and deep brownish-red or reddish-black, and the star effect is caused by inclusions of rutile that have the correct alignment to reflect light in a pattern forming a multi-rayed star. Most star garnets display a 4-rayed star, but 6-rayed stars are also sometimes seen. Star garnets are quite rare and have only been found in two places in the world: Idaho, USA, and India. Most of the members of the garnet family are cut as gemstones, or enjoyed as display specimens. Lesser quality material is commonly used as abrasives, such as in sandpaper.

SYSTEM	Isometric
COLOR	Red, orange, yellow, green, blue (rarely), purple, brown, black, colorless
HARDNESS	6.5-7.5
ENVIRONMENT	Metamorphic rocks, pegmatites, serpentines
OCCURRENCES	Africa, Australia, Canada, China, India, Italy, Mexico, Pakistan, Russia; Arizona, California, Colorado, Idaho, Maine, North Carolina, Vermont, Washington, USA
VALUE	$20+ per specimen

Metaphysical Properties

A Shamanistic mineral that may assist the user in meditation, spiritual traveling, and exploring the users deep psyche. An ideal crystal for enhancing the users innate desire to use kindness as opposed to harshness.

Pyrope

Metaphysical Properties: A protector of the body and psychic powers within the user. Its main concern is nourishing that connection and providing synchronicity with the entire human consciousness.

Spessartine

Metaphysical Properties: A crystal that selects users who are ready for their consciousness to ascend into higher levels of growth than previously experienced. Provides enhancements to the user's ability to calculate and analyze for the sake of discovery and exploration.

Grossular

Metaphysical Properties: Stability within the user may be granted in the face of challenge and when dealing with aggressive people. This crystal may also facilitate a sense of willingness to cooperate within the user to further along decisions and actions that must take place when dealing with others.

Andradite

Metaphysical Properties: Enhances qualities generally associated with males, or of masculine stereotypes within the user—qualities such as stamina, courage, or aggressiveness. Another form of this garnet is called *demantoid*, which can stimulate high quantities of energy from within the user.

Uvarovite

Metaphysical Properties: Provides the user with a sense of inner peace within solitude; to feel comfortable with the self without outside noises or visual media. Also bestows a sense of camaraderie and cooperation within relationships that the user may have.

Garnet-Pyrope

ASTROLOGICAL SIGN

Cancer

Leo

VIBRATES TO
THE NUMBER
5

RULES

Root

Crown

Pyrope garnet crystals on matrix from Arizona, small cabinet.
Photo courtesy of Patti Polk collection.

Garnet-Spessartine

ASTROLOGICAL SIGN

Aquarius

VIBRATES TO THE NUMBER(S)

1 & 7

RULES

Root

Sacral

Solar Plexus

Spessartine garnet crystals on smoky quartz crystals with microcline from China, small cabinet.
Photo courtesy of Larry Michon collection.

Garnet-Grossular

ASTROLOGICAL SIGN

Cancer

VIBRATES TO THE NUMBER(S)

2 & 6

RULES

Solar Plexus

Heart

Grossular garnet crystals on matrix from Mexico, small cabinet.
Photo courtesy of Patti Polk collection.

Garnet-Andradite

ASTROLOGICAL SIGN

Aries

RULES

Root

VIBRATES TO
THE NUMBER

4

Andradite garnet crystals on matrix from Arizona, small cabinet.
Photo courtesy of Patti Polk collection.

Garnet-Uvarovite

ASTROLOGICAL SIGN

Aquarius

RULES

Heart

Solar Plexus

VIBRATES TO
THE NUMBER

7

Uvarovite crystals on matrix from Russia, cabinet.
Photo courtesy of Larry Michon collection.

Glauberite

ASTROLOGICAL SIGN

♍

Virgo

RULES

Crown

VIBRATES TO THE NUMBER

4

Glauberite crystal cluster from Camp Verde, Arizona, USA, miniature. Photo courtesy of Patti Polk collection.

Glauberite is sodium calcium sulfate and forms as tabular, prismatic, dipyramidal crystals sometimes with rounded edges and striated faces. Glauberite is a common constituent of salt deposits and is transparent to translucent with a vitreous to greasy luster, and may develop a white powdery coating on its surface over time with exposure to air. Glauberite often forms in desert climates and is associated with halite, anhydrite, gypsum, and thenardite. Glauberite will dissolve slowly in water and alter to gypsum over time. Glauberite has a number of commercial uses such as a mordant to fix dyes and occasionally as a medicine. Glauberite is mainly of interest to mineral specimen collectors.

SYSTEM	Monoclinic
COLOR	Colorless, white, pale yellow, pale gray
HARDNESS	2.5-3
ENVIRONMENT	Evaporate deposits of sedimentary rocks
OCCURRENCES	Austria, France, Russia, Spain; Arizona, California, New Mexico, Texas, USA
VALUE	$5+ per specimen

Metaphysical Properties

Glauberite provides clarity and focus, especially to the tired or anxious mind. Used also as a grounding device that enhances one's feelings of comfort and safety upon returning home after a long day at work.

Goethite

ASTROLOGICAL SIGN

♈

Aries

VIBRATES TO
THE NUMBER

44

RULES

Sexual/
Creative

Third Eye

Botryoidal goethite on quartz
from Graves Mountain, Georgia,
USA, miniature. Photo courtesy of
Chris Whitney-Smith collection.

Goethite is iron hydroxide and forms as individual crystals in small, flattened blades and plates, or is finely acicular with a velvety appearance. Most often in botryoidal, reniform, or stalactitic aggregates of radiating ball-like crystals. Also granular, concretionary, oolitic, and in veins or earthy masses. Goethite often assumes the shape of other minerals forming a pseudomorph in place of the original mineral or as a coating above it. Goethite is opaque with a submetallic to silky luster, and a common Earth-forming mineral. Goethite may occasionally be radiantly iridescent with a multicolored rainbow-like display of colors such as the beautiful specimens from Graves Mountain in Georgia, USA. Goethite is named after Johann Wolfgang von Goethe (1749-1832), the famed German poet, philosopher, biologist, and mineral enthusiast and is a popular mineral specimen for collectors.

Iridescent botryoidal goethite from
Graves Mountain, Georgia, USA,
small cabinet.
Photo courtesy of Patti Polk collection.

Metaphysical Properties

Goethite assists in allowing the user to express and experience grief while providing a sense of grounding, knowing that the feelings of grief will indeed end. Goethite allows for the user to become more compassionate toward those who are grieving, and to share experiences of emotional healing.

SYSTEM	Orthorhombic
COLOR	Yellow, yellowish-brown, dark brown, black
HARDNESS	5-5.5
ENVIRONMENT	Hydrothermal replacement deposits
OCCURRENCES	Canada, Czechoslovakia, England, France, Germany, Russia; Colorado, Georgia, Michigan, USA
VALUE	$15+ per specimen

Gold

ASTROLOGICAL SIGN

♌

Leo

VIBRATES TO
THE NUMBER

2

Crystallized gold specimen from Ouray, Colorado, USA, thumbnail.
Photo courtesy of Patti Polk; Steve Willenburg collection.

RULES

Crown

Third Eye

Heart

Gold is a native element that forms rarely as small octahedral, cubic, and dodecahedral crystals and more commonly as grains, sheets, flakes, nuggets, and wires. Gold is opaque with a bright metallic luster and does not tarnish. Gold is malleable and ductile and has been a valuable and highly sought-after precious metal for coinage, jewelry, and other applications since long before the beginning of recorded history. The historical value of gold was rooted in its relatively easy handling, minting, and smelting; its resistance to corrosion, distinct color, and non-reactivity to other elements. Today, these same qualities have led to its continued use in corrosion resistant electrical connectors in all types of computerized devices (its chief industrial use). Gold is also used in infrared shielding, colored-glass production, gold leafing, and in tooth restoration. Certain gold salts are still used as anti-inflammatories in medicine.

SYSTEM	Isometric
COLOR	Golden or brassy yellow
HARDNESS	2.5-3
ENVIRONMENT	Hydrothermal replacement deposits, quartz veins, placer deposits
OCCURRENCES	Africa, Australia, Canada, Mexico; Alaska, Arizona, California, Colorado, USA
VALUE	$100+ per specimen

Metaphysical Properties

Gold prompts the user to see and retain their own inner beauty during the numerous events that must occur in life. It eases the sense of tiresome responsibility, promotes a sense of honor and happiness within the user, and enforces stability. Gold also assists the user in purification of the physical body and aids in the development of spiritual understanding.

Gypsum

ASTROLOGICAL SIGN

♈

Aries

VIBRATES TO
THE NUMBER

2

RULES

Root

Sacral

Ram's Horn gypsum crystals from
Mexico, miniature. Photo courtesy of
Patti Polk; Dick Moore collection.

Gypsum is sodium calcium sulfate, has a vitreous to silky luster, and occurs in a number of forms including clear tabular crystals that often appear as swallowtail or spearhead twins, transparent cleavable masses called *selenite* (see Selenite*)*; fibrous, elongated, twisted crystals known as *ram's horn*; fibrous elongated crystals known as *satin spar*; and rosettes with embedded grains of sand called *desert roses* or *gypsum flowers*. Desert roses are an opaque, rosette-shaped, bladed gypsum with an outer druse of sand or sand-included, and colored by the color of the included sand. The desert rose name can also be applied to barite desert roses (another related sulfate mineral), but barite is a harder mineral with higher density. Gypsum Flowers are also an opaque, rosette-shaped gypsum with spreading fibers that can include an outer druse, but the difference between desert roses and gypsum flowers is that desert roses look like roses, whereas gypsum flowers can form a myriad of shapes. Satin Spar forms as elongated, silky, fibrous, and translucent crystals with a pearly to milky luster that can occasionally exhibit some coloration. The *satin spar* name can also be applied to fibrous calcite (a related calcium mineral), although calcite is a harder mineral and feels greasier, waxier, or oilier to the touch.

Gypsum also takes the form of alabaster, in large, dense, granular, and compact waxy-looking masses, sometimes banded, that has been cut and sculpted as decorative stone since ancient Egypt. Today, gypsum is commercially mined and used as an ingredient in fertilizer, and as the main constituent in many forms of plaster, blackboard chalk and wallboard. Gypsum crystals are collected as display specimens and selenite is commonly used as a healing stone.

Desert Rose gypsum formation from Arizona, USA, small cabinet. Photo courtesy of Patti Polk collection.

Satin spar crystal from Mexico, cabinet specimen. Photo courtesy of Patti Polk collection.

Gypsum sand crystal from Mexico, small cabinet. Photo courtesy of Patti Polk collection.

Metaphysical Properties

Gypsum: Spurs action and banishes stagnation within the user to provoke progression and positive growth. On the opposite note, this crystal also maintains the user's wits when unexpected changes would normally cause internal chaos or discomfort. Gypsum is also considered a lucky stone and works to bring in an influence of abundance in a person's life.

SYSTEM	Monoclinic
COLOR	Colorless, white, gray, yellow, red, brown
HARDNESS	1.5-2
ENVIRONMENT	Hydrothermal replacement deposits, evaporates, sedimentary rocks
OCCURRENCES	Australia, Canada, Mexico, Peru, Romania, Spain; New Jersey, New York, Ohio, Oklahoma, Utah, USA
VALUE	$5+ per specimen

Halite

ASTROLOGICAL SIGN

Cancer

Pisces

**VIBRATES TO
THE NUMBER**

1

RULES

All
Chakras

Pink halite crystal cluster exhibiting
the hopper habit from Trona, California,
USA, cabinet specimen. Photo courtesy of
Patti Polk; Barbara Grill collection.

Halite is sodium chloride and forms as cubic crystals, often distorted with cavernous faces, "hopper" crystals, and as grains, crusts, and masses. Halite is transparent to translucent, has a vitreous luster and is sometimes fluorescent. Halite is most commonly known as "rock salt" and is used extensively in cooking as a flavor enhancer and is used in the curing process of a wide variety of foods such as bacon and fish. Halite commonly occurs with gypsum, thenardite, potash, and borax and is water-soluble. Candle holders carved from massive salt blocks from the Himalayas are often used as an air purifier when heated by a burning candle.

Well-formed halite crystal with color zoning from the PCA Mine, New Mexico, USA, small cabinet. Photo courtesy of Chris Whitney-Smith collection.

SYSTEM	Isometric
COLOR	Colorless, white, blue, pink, red, violet, yellow, gray, brown
HARDNESS	2-2.5
ENVIRONMENT	Evaporate deposits of chemical sedimentary rocks
OCCURRENCES	Austria, Germany, Poland, Sicily, Spain; California, Kansas, Michigan, New Mexico, New York, Utah, USA
VALUE	$5+ per specimen

Metaphysical Properties

The various colors of halite affect the user in different ways: colorless purifies the body's energy; violet helps to understand dreams; blue cleanses one's psychic abilities; yellow promotes self-discipline; pink uses love to guide the user away from harmful habits; the rest of the dark colors clears away negativity.

Hanksite

RULES

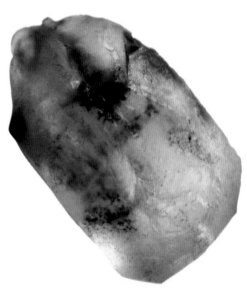

**All
Chakras**

Single hanksite crystal with inclusions from Searles
Lake, California, USA, thumbnail.
Photo courtesy of Patti Polk collection.

Hanksite is anhydrous sodium potassium chloride and is unusual, as it is one of only a handful of minerals that contain both carbonate and sulfate ion groups. Hanksite forms in large, stubby, prismatic, tabular crystals with pyramidal terminations and crystals should be kept lightly oiled to prevent them from evaporation over time. Hanksite is transparent to translucent and has a vitreous to dull luster and may fluoresce yellow under UV light. Hanksite is associated with halite, borax, trona, and aphthitalite in Searles Lake, California, and named for H. G. Hanks, an American geologist.

SYSTEM	Hexagonal
COLOR	Colorless, greenish-gray, pale yellow
HARDNESS	3-3.5
ENVIRONMENT	Lacustrine evaporate deposits
OCCURRENCES	Searles Lake, California, USA
VALUE	$5+ per specimen

Metaphysical Properties

Hanksite cleanses the body of pent-up anger and frustration so the user may continue to live their life with a greater sense of peace. This crystal may also ground the user into this physical plane and eliminate unnecessary or harmful internal energies.

Hematite

ASTROLOGICAL SIGN

♈

Aries

♒

Aquarius

VIBRATES TO THE NUMBER

9

RULES

Root

Hematite after marcasite pseudomorph crystals with captured grains of sand from the White Desert, Egypt, small cabinet.
Photo courtesy of Chris Whitney-Smith collection.

Hematite is iron oxide and forms as thick to thin tabular crystals, as rosettes "iron rose" or subparallel growths, striated, and also as botroyoidal, reniform, columnar, compact masses. Hematite may also form as a micaceous mass "specular," and sometimes has an iridescent surface. Hematite is opaque and heavy with a metallic luster and is weakly magnetic. Hematite is the main ore of iron and huge deposits of hematite are found in banded iron formations. Hematite can precipitate out of water and collect in layers at the bottom of a lake, spring, or other standing water. Hematite can also occur without water, however, usually as the result of volcanic activity. The earthy form of hematite, red ochre, has been used as a paint pigment since ancient times and is still used today as a polishing powder or rouge. Hard pieces of hematite were cut and faceted as small stones for jewelry making in the Victorian era and throughout history hematite has been carved into small figurines or intaglios.

Metaphysical Properties

Hematite can be used for mental attunement, memory enhancement, and for developing creative thinking. It assists in releasing limitations of the mind and helps the body to expel excessive heat while calming and balancing the physical nervous system.

Specular Hematite

The self-doubt of one's spiritual status (as being spiritual enough or not) will be subdued when using this mineral. A helpful tool when attempting to achieve spiritual growth.

SYSTEM	Hexagonal
COLOR	Red, reddish-brown, steel-gray, black
HARDNESS	5.5-6.5
ENVIRONMENT	Iron ore deposits, sedimentary deposits, metamorphic rocks
OCCURRENCES	Brazil, Canada, England, Italy, Switzerland; Arizona, Michigan, Minnesota, New York, Tennessee, USA
VALUE	$10+ per specimen

Hemimorphite

ASTROLOGICAL SIGN

♎︎
Libra

VIBRATES TO
THE NUMBER

4

Botryoidal blue hemimorphite on
matrix from China, cabinet.
Photo courtesy of Dr. Robert Lavinsky collection.

RULES

Heart

Throat

Third Eye

Crown

Transpersonal

Etheric

Hemimorphite is hydrous zinc silicate and forms in thin tabular crystals, fan-shaped aggregates of platy crystals, coxcomb groups, radiating crusts, and as mammillary, stalactitic, and compact masses. Hemimorphite is transparent to translucent, has a vitreous to silky luster, and is a minor ore of zinc. Hemimorphite fluoresces under UV light and is associated with smithsonite, gypsum, calcite, and hematite. Hemimorphite is generally collected as a display specimen and the blue-green plates are especially valued due to their vibrant and beautiful color.

SYSTEM	Orthorhombic
COLOR	Colorless, white, blue, blue-green, yellow, brown
HARDNESS	4.5-5
ENVIRONMENT	Oxidation zone of zinc and lead sulfide deposits
OCCURRENCES	China, England, Mexico, Russia; Colorado, Missouri, Montana, New Jersey, New Mexico, Pennsylvania, USA
VALUE	$15+ per specimen

Metaphysical Properties

Hemimorphite attunes the user to be aware of their own emotions, and allows the contemplation of those emotions to be supportive and compassionate as opposed to being judgmental or severe. Those interested in shamanistic travel may also find that this mineral allows for the user to connect with higher realms of knowledge.

Hemimorphite crystals on matrix with
a dusting of hematite on the crystals,
from Chihuahua, Mexico, small cabinet.
Photo courtesy of Dr. Robert Lavinsky collection.

Idocrase

ASTROLOGICAL SIGN

Sagittarius

Capricorn

**VIBRATES TO
THE NUMBER(S)**

2 & 3

Gemmy vesuvianite crystal cluster from Canada,
miniature. Photo courtesy of Dr. Robert Lavinsky collection.

RULES

**All
Chakras**

Idocrase is a calcium magnesium aluminum silicate that forms as stubby, prismatic crystals, as compact granular masses, and as columnar aggregates with finely striated faces. Idocrase is translucent to transparent and has a vitreous to resinous luster. Idocrase is more well known by the common name *vesuvianite*, which was originally discovered within included blocks adjacent to lavas on Mount Vesuvius, hence its name. Transparent crystals of vesuvianite are cut and faceted as gemstones for jewelry making and a massive jade-like variety of vesuvianite that comes from California is called *californite*.

SYSTEM	Tetragonal
COLOR	Brown, green, yellow, blue
HARDNESS	6.5
ENVIRONMENT	Contact metamorphic skarns, serpentinized ultramafic rocks
OCCURRENCES	Canada, Italy, Mexico, Norway, Pakistan, Switzerland; Arkansas, California, New Jersey, Oregon, Vermont, USA
VALUE	$25+ per specimen

Metaphysical Properties

Idocrase is a crystal of stability, encouragement, and positive thinking. Negative thoughts and their results will be banished from the body and mind upon use, and spiritual security while on the physical plane will be granted.

Kyanite

ASTROLOGICAL SIGN

♉

Taurus

♎

Libra

♈

Aries

VIBRATES TO THE NUMBER

4

RULES

All
Chakras

Single blue kyanite crystal
from Brazil, miniature.
Photo courtesy of Patti Polk collection.

Kyanite is an aluminum silicate that forms in elongated tabular crystals, rarely terminated, in groups of bladed crystal aggregates. Kyanite is transparent to translucent, splintery, and has a vitreous to pearly luster and is found in gneiss, mica schists, and amphibolites with garnet, staurolite, and micas. Kyanite is used primarily in refractory and ceramic products, including porcelain plumbing fixtures and dishware. It is also used in electronics, electrical insulators, spark plugs, and abrasives. Kyanite has been cut as a semi-precious gemstone, which may occasionally display cat's eye chatoyancy. Color varieties include a recently discovered orange kyanite from Tanzania with the orange color being due to the inclusion of small amounts of manganese in the crystal.

Black kyanite crystal spray
from Brazil, miniature.
Photo courtesy of Patti Polk collection.

SYSTEM	Triclinic
COLOR	Blue, white, colorless, gray, green, orange, black
HARDNESS	Lengthwise, 4-5; Crosswise, 6-7
ENVIRONMENT	Peltic rocks, metamorphic rocks, pegmatites
OCCURRENCES	Africa, Brazil, Switzerland; California, Georgia, North Carolina, USA
VALUE	$10+ per specimen

Metaphysical Properties

Kyanite prevents the accumulation of negative energy or vibrations within the user; that negativity can then be dispelled through meditation. Connectivity between the user and the universe (all planes) can then be allowed, making this crystal a valuable tool in daily life.

Lazulite

ASTROLOGICAL SIGN

Sagittarius

Gemini

**VIBRATES TO
THE NUMBER**

7

RULES

Third Eye

Lazulite crystals in quartz from Graves
Mountain, Georgia, USA, cabinet specimen.
Photo courtesy of Patti Polk, Travis Hartins collection.

Lazulite is a phosphate of magnesium, iron, and aluminum and forms as pointed or wedge-shaped, prismatic, bipyramidal crystals often embedded in matrix, and as granular masses. Lazulite is transparent to opaque with a vitreous luster and occurs with quartz, muscovite, rutile, kyanite, garnet, and corundum. When sufficiently transparent, lazulite is cut and polished as a gemstone for use in jewelry making. Due to its rich blue color, it may be confused with azurite, lazurite, and lapis lazuli.

SYSTEM	Monoclinic
COLOR	Deep blue to medium blue, greenish-blue
HARDNESS	5-6
ENVIRONMENT	Metamorphic rocks, pegmatites, quartz veins
OCCURRENCES	Austria, Brazil, Canada, Switzerland; California, Georgia, USA
VALUE	$20+ per specimen

Metaphysical Properties

Lazulite brings clarity and purity of energy from the universe to be instilled within the user. Psychic abilities will thus be enhanced, making old problems seem less daunting and suddenly solvable.

L

Lepidolite

ASTROLOGICAL SIGN

♎
Libra

VIBRATES TO THE NUMBER

8

RULES

All Chakras

Scaly, lilac-colored lepidolite aggregate
from Brazil, cabinet size.
Photo courtesy of Patti Polk; Dick Moore collection.

Lepidolite is a basic fluorosilicate of potassium, lithium, and aluminum that belongs to the mica group. Lepidolite forms rarely as hexagonal, sharp, well-developed crystals, and commonly in scaly or platy aggregates, and masses. Laminae lepidolite is tough and elastic, and is translucent to transparent with a pearly luster. Lepidolite is an ore of lithium and occurs with spodumene, amblygonite, quartz, tourmaline, and feldspar, and is one of the major sources of the rare alkali metals rubidium and caesium. Lepidolite is a soothing stone to keep nearby, as it is an ore of lithium and helps to balance brain chemistry.

SYSTEM	Monoclinic
COLOR	Pink, lilac, yellow, gray-green
HARDNESS	2.5-3
ENVIRONMENT	Granite pegmatites
OCCURRENCES	Australia, Brazil, Canada, Japan, Russia, Sweden; California, New Mexico, South Dakota, USA
VALUE	$10+ per specimen

Metaphysical Properties

Lepidolite helps the user through transitions in life that seem frightening or unwelcomed. This mineral allows for openness of mind to provide a smooth sense of adaptability during moments of change. Lepidolite is one of the most calming of all collectible minerals and is useful in treating mentally agitated states or nervous conditions.

Magnetite

ASTROLOGICAL SIGN

♈
Aries

♑
Capricorn

♒
Aquarius

♍
Virgo

VIBRATES TO THE NUMBER

4

RULES

All Chakras

Magnetite crystals on matrix from Germany, cabinet.
Photo courtesy of Dr. Robert Lavinsky collection.

Magnetite is an iron oxide that belongs to the spinel group. Magnetite forms as octahedrons or dodecahedrons with striated faces, also as masses, granular, or occasionally as lamellar crystals. Magnetite is opaque with a metallic luster and occurs in a variety of environments. Magnetite is the most magnetic of all the naturally occurring minerals on Earth and naturally magnetized pieces of magnetite, called *lodestone*, will attract small pieces of iron, which is how ancient peoples first discovered the property of magnetism. Lodestones were used as an early form of a magnetic compass. Magnetite typically carries the dominant magnetic signature in rocks, and so it has been a critical tool in paleomagnetism, a science important in understanding plate tectonics and the geologic history of rock formation. Magnetite is an important ore of iron.

Magnetite crystals in nephrite jade
that have been 24k gold-plated
and polished as a cabochon, from
California, miniature.
Photo courtesy of Patti Polk; Kevin Kessler collection.

SYSTEM	Isometric
COLOR	Black, gray, brownish
HARDNESS	5.5-6.5
ENVIRONMENT	Igneous rocks, sedimentary rocks, metamorphic rocks
OCCURRENCES	Africa, Germany, Italy, Russia, Switzerland; Arkansas, New Jersey, New York, Pennsylvania, Utah, Wyoming, USA
VALUE	$5+ per specimen

Metaphysical Properties

Magnetite temporarily aligns all of the elements of the body to provide inner harmony and clear thinking. Magnetite facilitates grounding and balancing with the Earth energies and enhances the ability to manifest that which one desires.

Malachite

ASTROLOGICAL SIGN

♑

Capricorn

♏

Scorpio

VIBRATES TO
THE NUMBER

9

Malachite crystal
cluster from Namibia,
Africa, small cabinet.
Photo courtesy of Dr. Robert
Lavinsky collection.

Malachite stalactitic cluster from
the Congo, Africa, small cabinet.
Photo courtesy of Mike Keim collection.

RULES

Solar Plexus

Heart

Malachite is a basic copper carbonate and commonly forms as fibrous, silky crusts; radiating aggregates; stalactitic, botroyoidal, or reniform masses with internal concentric banding; and fine acicular sprays. Individual crystals are rare but do occur as slender, sometimes twinned, prismatic crystals. Malachite is opaque to translucent and has an adamantine to silky luster. Malachite usually results from the weathering of copper ores and is often found together with azurite, goethite, and calcite. Malachite has historically been an important mineral to mankind and archeological evidence indicates that the mineral has been mined and smelted to obtain copper at Timna Valley in Israel for more than 3,000 years. Since then, malachite has been used as an ornamental stone, as a gemstone, and as a paint pigment in green paints from antiquity until about 1800 when it was replaced with new synthetic pigments. Malachite mineral specimens are collected and prized for their beautiful color and forms, and malachite is commonly used today in the making of beads and cabochons for use in jewelry.

SYSTEM	Monoclinic
COLOR	Dark emerald green to light green
HARDNESS	3.5-4
ENVIRONMENT	Oxidation zone of copper deposits
OCCURRENCES	Africa, Australia, Mexico, Russia; Arizona, Michigan, Nevada, Utah, USA
VALUE	$20+ per specimen

Metaphysical Properties

Malachite is a cleansing mineral that removes blockages to allow for the users' wishes to fully manifest themselves to the desired result. Malachite is a stone of transformation, assisting in the ability to adapt to changing situations and in clarifying the emotional state.

Millerite

ASTROLOGICAL SIGN

♏

Scorpio

RULES

Solar Plexus

VIBRATES TO THE NUMBER

4

Geode containing acicular millerite needles with calcite from Wisconsin, USA, small cabinet. Photo courtesy of Dr. Robert Lavinsky collection.

Millerite is a nickel sulfide mineral and forms as hair-like, slender, brassy crystals, often in radiating groups, and as columnar tufted coatings. Millerite is heavy, opaque, has a metallic luster, and is commonly found as radiating clusters of acicular needle-like crystals in cavities of sulfide rich limestone and dolomite, or in geodes. It is also found in nickel-iron meteorites, such as CK carbonaceous chondrites. Millerite is one of the richest ores for nickel, but due to its rarity, it is not mined commercially and is only commonly used as an attractive display specimen for collectors.

SYSTEM	Hexagonal
COLOR	Brassy yellow
HARDNESS	3-3.5
ENVIRONMENT	Hydrothermal replacement deposits
OCCURRENCES	Australia, France, Germany, Italy, Romania, Wales; Iowa, Kentucky, Missouri, Wisconsin, USA
VALUE	$50+ per specimen

Metaphysical Properties

Millerite assists the user in seeing the world through open eyes so that opportunities and changes may seem less daunting and more exciting—as moments that may bring goodness as opposed to feelings of imbalance. Provides awareness to such opportunities, and lessens one's abrasiveness when confronting others with suggestions.

Mimetite

ASTROLOGICAL SIGN

♑

Capricorn

RULES

Heart

VIBRATES TO
THE NUMBER

4

Glassy spherical mimetite with wulfenite on matrix from the Rowley Mine, Arizona, USA, miniature. Photo courtesy of Chris Whitney-Smith collection.

Mimetite is lead chloroarsenate and forms as slender to thick, hexagonal prismatic crystals, sometimes with curved faces, often in groups or aggregates; also globular, reniform, and as mammillary crusts. Mimetite is transparent to translucent with a resinous to adamantine luster and is found in association with lead and arsenic minerals, including those minerals with which it forms a series. Some associated minerals include calcite, galena, pyromorphite, smithsonite, vanadinite, and wulfenite. Industrially, mimetite is a minor ore of lead. The chief use of mimetite is as a collector's specimen, often creating attractive botryoidal crusts on the surface of the host matrix. Though mimetite is found in prismatic crystal forms, it is not used as a gemstone due to its softness.

Sugary yellow mimetite from the Ojuela Mine, Mexico, miniature.
Photo courtesy of Dr. Robert Lavinsky collection.

SYSTEM	Monoclinic
COLOR	Pale to bright yellow, yellow-orange, brown, colorless
HARDNESS	3.5
ENVIRONMENT	Oxidation zone of lead and zinc deposits
OCCURRENCES	Africa, Australia, China, Czechoslovakia, England, Mexico, Saxony; Arizona, Pennsylvania, USA
VALUE	$20+ per specimen

Metaphysical Properties

Mimetite provides a balance between the user and the surrounding world, creating a harmony within the inner chaos the user may be feeling. It may also create a barrier of sorts between the user and the tiresome demands of the world, so that the user does not feel exhausted after performing necessary tasks.

Moldavite

Aries

Cancer

Gem quality, bottle-green discoidal tektite on pebble conglomerate matrix from Czech Republic, small cabinet. Photo courtesy of Dr. Robert Lavinsky collection.

RULES

All Chakras

VIBRATES TO THE NUMBER

9

Moldavite is composed of silicon aluminum oxide and one of the rarest materials on earth. Moldavite is a form of natural glass called a tektite that formed from a massive meteorite impact in central Europe about 14.7 million years ago. Moldavite is transparent to semi-opaque, and has a vitreous luster. Tektites are found in a number of regions in the world, but the name Moldavite is reserved for the tektites found in the Moldau River region of the Czech Republic. Isotope analysis of European moldavite tektite samples have shown a beryllium-10 isotope composition similar to the composition of Australasian tektites (australites) and Ivory Coast tektites (ivorites). Their similarity in beryllium-10 isotope composition indicates that moldavites, australites, and ivorites consist of near surface and loosely consolidated terrestrial sediments melted by hypervelocity impacts. There are typically two grades of moldavite: high quality, often referred to as museum grade, and regular grade. Museum and regular grade moldavites can be told apart by their appearance. The regular grade pieces are usually darker and more saturated in their green color, and the surface is seen as closely spaced pitting or weathering. This type sometimes appears to have been broken apart from a larger chunk. The museum grade has a distinct fern-like pattern and is much more gemmy or translucent than the regular grade. There is usually a fairly big difference in the price between the two. High-quality moldavite stones are often used in handcrafted jewelry or as talismans.

SYSTEM	Amorphous
COLOR	Mossy green, bottle green
HARDNESS	5.5
ENVIRONMENT	Meteoric impact craters
OCCURRENCES	Africa, Austria, Czech Republic, Germany
VALUE	$40+ per specimen

Metaphysical Properties

Moldavite aids in accessing higher dimensional galactic energies to bring in thought patterns and vibrations for use on this planet; also an encourager to gather knowledge from all planes to have a solid and well-rounded understanding of the universe.

Muscovite

Muscovite mica cluster
from North Carolina, USA,
small cabinet.
Photo courtesy of Patti Polk; Dick
Moore collection.

Muscovite is basic potassium aluminum silicate and a member of the mica group. Muscovite forms as tabular crystals, often with a hexagonal outline, sometimes with striations on the prism faces; also as foliated, scaly, lamellar masses. Muscovite is translucent to transparent, has a vitreous to pearly luster, and is flexible and elastic when cleaved into thin, lamellar sheets. The green, chromium-rich variety is called *fuchsite*, which is often included with ruby crystals and is in high demand as a gemstone and metaphysical stone. Muscovite is the most common mica, found in granites, pegmatites, gneisses, and schists, and as a contact metamorphic rock or as a secondary mineral resulting from the alteration of topaz, feldspar, kyanite, and other minerals. In pegmatites, it is often found in immense sheets that are commercially valuable. In the past, Muscovite has been historically used as a substitute for glass in windowpanes and as a lampshade due to its fire resistant properties. Muscovite is in demand for the manufacture of fireproofing and insulating materials, as a filler in industrial products, and as a dry lubricant.

Massive fuchsite from
Brazil, small cabinet.
Photo courtesy of Patti Polk collection.

SYSTEM	Monoclinic
COLOR	Colorless, silvery-white, gray, pale yellow, greenish, pink, brown
HARDNESS	2-2.5
ENVIRONMENT	Metamorphic rocks, pegmatites, plutonic igneous rocks
OCCURRENCES	Brazil, Canada, India, Switzerland; Colorado, Massachusetts, North Carolina, South Dakota, Utah, Virginia, USA
VALUE	$10+ per specimen

Metaphysical Properties

Muscovite provides self-confidence within the user, and reduces feelings of insecurity and self-doubt. Muscovite also maintains the user's integrity after relationships end so that the user can continue to live life measurably unhindered.

Natrolite

ASTROLOGICAL SIGN

Cancer

♓
Pisces

♏
Scorpio

VIBRATES TO THE NUMBER

6

RULES

Third Eye

Crown

Geode with an acicular natrolite spray
from India, cabinet specimen.
Photo courtesy of Patti Polk; Dick Moore collection.

Natrolite is hydrous sodium aluminum silicate that forms as slender, prismatic crystals with vertical striations, acicular, in radiating groups, often lining cavities in volcanic rocks. Natrolite is transparent to translucent, has a vitreous to pearly luster, may be fluorescent, and is a member of the zeolite group. Natrolite derives from the Greek word *nitron*, meaning "niter," and *lithos*, meaning "stone," in allusion to the composition of the mineral. Natrolite is a mineral of interest only to scientists and collectors, as it has no applicable commercial value.

SYSTEM	Orthorhombic
COLOR	Colorless, white, yellowish, pale pink
HARDNESS	5-5.5
ENVIRONMENT	Cavities of igneous basaltic rocks, nepheline syenites
OCCURRENCES	Brazil, Canada, France, Greenland, Ireland, India, Italy, Russia; California, Montana, New Jersey, Oregon, USA
VALUE	$10+ per specimen

Metaphysical Properties

Natrolite is a crystal with tender-hearted abilities that is used to soften the process of rebirth and make the user's new life less startling from the experience of starting over. Both before and after this rebirth, this crystal promotes contact with the spiritual planes to ensure continuous contact with the spiritual realms.

Neptunite

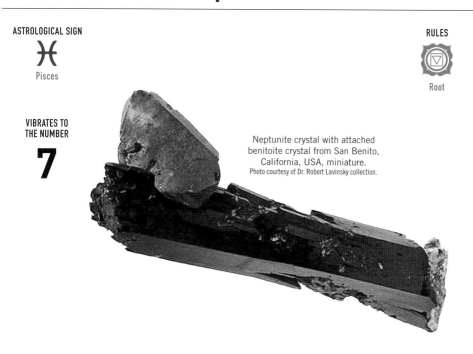

ASTROLOGICAL SIGN

♓
Pisces

RULES

Root

VIBRATES TO THE NUMBER

7

Neptunite crystal with attached benitoite crystal from San Benito, California, USA, miniature.
Photo courtesy of Dr. Robert Lavinsky collection.

Neptunite is a complex titanosilicate of sodium, potassium, iron, and manganese and forms as elongated, prismatic crystals with pointed terminations. Neptunite is opaque to translucent with a vitreous luster. Neptunite was first described in 1893 for an occurrence in the Narssârssuk pegmatite of West Greenland. It is also found in natrolite veins in glaucophane schist within serpentinite in San Benito County, California, USA, in association with benitonite, an extremely rare mineral. It also occurs in Mont Saint-Hilaire, Quebec, and in the Kola Peninsula of Russia, and is named for Neptune, the Roman god of the sea. Neptunite is quite rare and much sought after by collectors of distinctive minerals.

SYSTEM	Monoclinic
COLOR	Black with dark red reflections
HARDNESS	5-6
ENVIRONMENT	Nepheline syenite pegmatites, altered serpentinites
OCCURRENCES	Greenland, Russia; California, USA
VALUE	$100+ per specimen

Metaphysical Properties

Neptunite assists the user in solving problems that the user cannot otherwise conquer or find solutions for. Also can be used as a helper in accomplishing both long and short-term goals and provides stability in the home environment.

Okenite

ASTROLOGICAL SIGN

↗
Sagittarius

♍
Virgo

**VIBRATES TO
THE NUMBER**

7

RULES

Crown

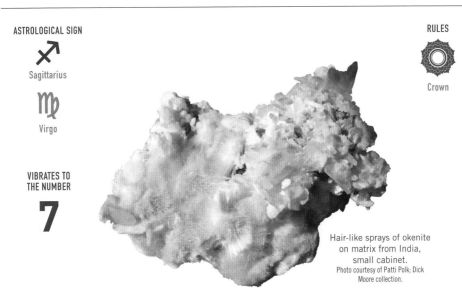

Hair-like sprays of okenite
on matrix from India,
small cabinet.
Photo courtesy of Patti Polk; Dick
Moore collection.

Okenite is hydrous calcium silicate hydroxide and is usually associated with zeolites. It most commonly is found as small white "cotton ball" formations within basalt geodes. These formations are clusters of straight, radiating, fibrous crystals that are both bendable and fragile. Okenite is transparent to translucent and has a vitreous to pearly luster. Minerals associated with okenite include apophyllite, gyrolite, prehnite, chalcedony, and many of the others of the zeolite group.

If you are looking to purchase okenite and see colorful specimens of okenite from China or India for sale, these are fake—the bright colors are artificial dyes added to the okenite.

Metaphysical Properties

Okenite is a Barrier Harmonizer crystal. Barrier crystals have powerful abilities to help us focus and amplify our efforts to keep undesirable elements out of our lives. Its crystalline structure gives it strength in all directions, allowing it to provide barriers to attack from all directions simultaneously. Okenite also encourages truthfulness from the user and to allow the truthfulness of others to be less harsh or intimidating to hear.

SYSTEM	Triclinic
COLOR	White to slightly yellow, bluish-white
HARDNESS	4.5-5
ENVIRONMENT	Amygdules in basalts
OCCURRENCES	Canada, Chile, Greenland, India, Ireland, New Zealand; Arizona, North Carolina, Oregon, Utah, Virginia, USA
VALUE	$40+ per specimen

Olivine

Olivine var. peridot crystal cluster
from Pakistan, thumbnail.
Photo courtesy of Chris Whitney-Smith collection.

The mineral olivine is a magnesium iron silicate and a common mineral in the Earth's composition. It is a type of nesosilicate or orthosilicate and the ratio of magnesium and iron varies between the two endmembers of the solid solution series: forsterite and fayalite. Olivine forms as stubby, prismatic crystals or rounded grains, usually in granular aggregates. Olivine is transparent to translucent with a vitreous luster. Most olivine is the variety *forsterite* that includes the gemstone known as *peridot*. Peridot has been used widely since ancient times as a semi-precious stone and today is generally cut and faceted for use in jewelry making. Olivine has also been discovered in meteorites called pallasites (a mix of iron-nickel and olivine), as well as in asteroid 25143 Itokawa.

Single olivine var. peridot crystal from
San Carlos, Arizona, USA, thumbnail.
Photo courtesy of Patti Polk collection.

SYSTEM	Orthorhombic
COLOR	Olive-green, yellow-green, brownish-green
HARDNESS	6.5-7
ENVIRONMENT	Common in gabbro, basalt, metamorphic rocks
OCCURRENCES	Brazil, Burma, Egypt, Italy, Norway, Russia; Arizona, California, New Mexico, USA
VALUE	$15+ per specimen

Metaphysical Properties

Peridot generates a warm and friendly vibration while also providing the user with a protective force field around the body and spirit. Peridot also cleanses the heart and solar plexus chakras, bringing the user greater open-mindedness both in terms of intellectual pursuits and in personal relationships.

Petalite

ASTROLOGICAL SIGN

Leo

VIBRATES TO THE NUMBER

7

RULES

Third Eye

Crown

Petalite crystal cluster from Afghanistan, small cabinet.
Photo courtesy of Dr. Robert Lavinsky collection.

Colorless faceted petalite crystal from Afghanistan, micromount.
Photo courtesy of Patti Polk; Lamont Latham collection.

Petalite, also known as *castorite*, is a lithium aluminium phyllosilicate mineral and a member of the feldspathoid group. Petalite forms as tabular or columnar prismatic crystals or in cleavage masses. Petalite is transparent to translucent with a vitreous to pearly luster. Petalite is an important ore of lithium and commonly found in association with spodumene, lepidolite, and tourmaline. The colorless varieties are often cut and faceted as gemstones. The first important economic application for petalite was as a raw material for glass-ceramic cooking ware and it has also been used as a raw material for ceramic glazes.

SYSTEM	Monoclinic
COLOR	Colorless, white, gray
HARDNESS	6-6.5
ENVIRONMENT	Lithium-bearing pegmatites
OCCURRENCES	Afghanistan, Africa, Australia, Brazil, Burma, Canada, Italy, Pakistan, Sweden; California, Maine, North Carolina, Wyoming, USA
VALUE	$40+ per specimen

Metaphysical Properties

Petalite may assist the user with clairaudience, as well as hearing advice given by one's spirit guardians beyond the physical plane. This crystal also provides retention of information received during meditation.

Phenakite

ASTROLOGICAL SIGN

♊

Gemini

RULES

Third Eye

Crown

**VIBRATES TO
THE NUMBER**

9

Phenakite twinned crystal from Mt. Antero, Colorado, USA, thumbnail.
Photo courtesy of Dr. Robert Lavinsky collection.

Phenakite, also known as *phenacite*, is a fairly rare nesosilicate mineral consisting of beryllium orthosilicate that forms as short to long, rhombohedral prismatic crystals, striated lengthwise and often penetration-twinned. Phenakite is transparent to translucent with a vitreous, glassy luster. Phenakite is often mistaken for quartz, but it is much harder and has different twinned forms. Phenakite often occurs in mica schists with quartz, beryl, apatite, and topaz. Water-clear crystals are sometimes faceted as gemstones.

SYSTEM	Hexagonal
COLOR	Colorless, white, yellow, pink, brown
HARDNESS	7.5-8
ENVIRONMENT	High temperature pegmatite veins, mica schists
OCCURRENCES	Brazil, Italy, Norway, Russia; Colorado, New Hampshire, Maine, Virginia, USA
VALUE	$50+ per specimen

Metaphysical Properties

Phenakite can provide total body cleansing as well as allow for connection between the user and the psychic plane. This crystal also amplifies the healing effects of other healing crystals within the user's vicinity.

Prehnite

ASTROLOGICAL SIGN

♎

Libra

RULES

▽

Solar Plexus

✡

Heart

VIBRATES TO
THE NUMBER

5

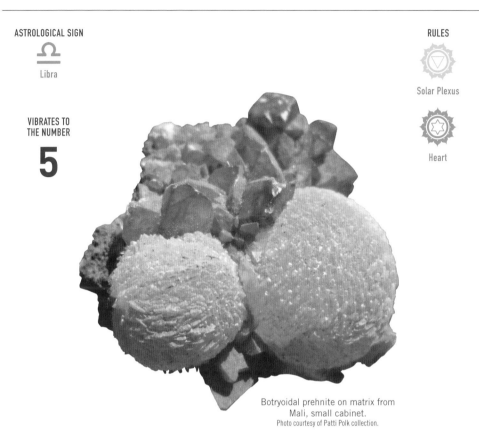

Botryoidal prehnite on matrix from
Mali, small cabinet.
Photo courtesy of Patti Polk collection.

Prehnite is an inosilicate of calcium and aluminium and generally forms mainly as reniform, mammillary, or stalactitic masses. Crystals are intergrown in botroyoidal masses, with ridged surfaces, and displaying edges of curving crystals. Individual crystals are rare and usually microscopic when found. Prehnite is translucent to almost transparent with a vitreous to waxy luster. Prehnite is a fairly common mineral found in many localities usually accompanied with zeolites, datolite, calcite, apophyllite, stilbite, laumontite, and heulandite. Prehnite frequently occurs in veins and cavities of basaltic rocks, and sometimes in granites, syenites, or gneisses. If transparent enough, prehnite can occasionally be cut as a gemstone, otherwise it is mainly of interest to collectors of mineral specimens.

Gemmy botryoidal prehnite crystal
mass from Tanzania, Africa, thumbnail.
Photo courtesy of Mike Keim collection.

Metaphysical Properties

When used for one's spiritual advancement, prehnite enhances the user's ability to visualize and prepare for the aftermath of such advancement that may arise on the physical plane. Also, a mineral helpful in aiding productive and fruitful growth during meditation.

SYSTEM	Orthorhombic
COLOR	Colorless, white, light green, yellow green, green, gray
HARDNESS	6-6.5
ENVIRONMENT	Basaltic rocks, metamorphic rocks
OCCURRENCES	Africa, Canada, France, India, Italy, Mali, Spain; Connecticut, Michigan, New Jersey, Virginia, USA
VALUE	$15+ per specimen

Proustite

ASTROLOGICAL SIGN

Aquarius

Leo

VIBRATES TO THE NUMBER

7

RULES

Root

Proustite crystal on quartz from Germany, miniature.
Photo courtesy of Dr. Robert Lavinsky collection.

Proustite is silver arsenic sulfide and is also know as "Ruby Silver." Proustite occurs as poorly formed prismatic rhombohedral crystals, striated, and often twinned; also as compact masses. Proustite is transparent to translucent and has an adamantine luster when fresh, but may become dull and semi-opaque when exposed to light and air over time. Proustite is an ore of silver and is often associated with native silver, quartz, and calcite in low temperature hydrothermal veins. Proustite is highly prized by collectors for its beautiful blood-red color and distinctive specimen display qualities.

SYSTEM	Hexagonal
COLOR	Scarlet red, vermillion red, blood red
HARDNESS	2-2.5
ENVIRONMENT	Low temperature hydrothermal veins
OCCURRENCES	Canada, Chile, Germany, Mexico; California, Colorado, Idaho, Nevada, USA
VALUE	$50+ per specimen

Metaphysical Properties

Proustite absorbs the user's negativity to the point where the crystal's physical appearance may be warped from siphoning such emotionally poisonous energies. A true stone of change, proustite allows for the user to accept change and transition smoothly into it.

Pyrite

ASTROLOGICAL SIGN

♌

Leo

RULES

Solar Plexus

VIBRATES TO
THE NUMBER

3

Pyrite crystal cluster from Peru, cabinet size.
Photo courtesy of Patti Polk collection.

The mineral pyrite (or iron pyrite), also known as "fool's gold," is an iron sulfide that forms as cubes, pyritohedrons, and octahedrons with parallel striations on its faces; also as concretions, mammillary and stalactitic nodules, massive and granular aggregates, and sometimes as a pseudomorph after organic fossil remains such as pyritized ammonites. Pyrite is opaque and has a metallic luster that may develop an iridescent yellowish-brown film. One of the most unusual varieties of pyrite are the disc-shaped pyrite "suns," also known as pyrite dollars, which exhibit striations radiating out from the center like rays of the sun. These unique specimens are recovered from underground coal mines near Sparta, Illinois, where they occur in narrow, compacted seams of slate interbedded in 300-million-year-old Pennsylvanian Period coal deposits. The origin of pyrite suns has been a subject of debate for many years and some authorities have speculated that they originated as fossils that were subsequently replaced with pyrite, but the current consensus is that they are concretions that spread out under pressure and were forced to grow in a laterally compressed, radiating manner in the seams of slate.

Pyrite is an abundant and widespread mineral and usually found associated with other sulfides or oxides in quartz veins, sedimentary rock, and metamorphic rock. Pyrite has been used in the manufacture of sulfuric acid and can be an indicator of gold deposits, but is mainly collected today as an attractive mineral specimen.

Pyrite cubes with quartz crystals
from Peru, cabinet size.
Photo courtesy of Patti Polk, Kevin Kessler collection.

Pyrite "sun" or "sand dollar" concretion from Sparta,
Illinois, USA, small cabinet. Photo courtesy of Patti Polk collection.

Metaphysical Properties

Pyrite is a highly protective mineral whose force field can shield negative energies from coming close to the user. Pyrite may also remind the user of pleasant memories concerning love, relationships, and friendships that enhance the user's daily mood and aid in repelling negativity.

SYSTEM	Isometric
COLOR	Brassy yellow, brownish-yellow
HARDNESS	6-6.5
ENVIRONMENT	Common in plutonic, volcanic, sedimentary and metamorphic rocks
OCCURRENCES	England, Germany, Italy, Mexico, Peru, Spain; Arizona, Colorado, Illinois, Pennsylvania, Utah, USA
VALUE	$10+ per specimen

Pyrolusite

ASTROLOGICAL SIGN

Leo

RULES

Root

VIBRATES TO
THE NUMBER

1

Crown

Pyrolusite cluster from Mexico, small cabinet.
Photo courtesy of Patti Polk; Dick Moore collection.

Pyrolusite is manganese dioxide and forms rarely as stubby prismatic crystals, more commonly as fibrous, acicular, radiating, concretionary aggregates or earthy masses. Pyrolusite is opaque with a metallic to dull luster and is an important ore of manganese. Pyrolusite occurs with manganite, hollandite, goethite, and hematite under oxidizing conditions in hydrothermal deposits and as a chemical precipitate in bogs or stagnant bodies of water. Historically, pyrolusite has had many uses including as an oxidizing agent in the preparation of chlorine, a decolorizer in the making of glass to remove unwanted tints, an ingredient in the making of alloys, and as a paint pigment. Today, pyrolusite is generally collected as an interesting display specimen.

SYSTEM	Tetragonal
COLOR	Steel-gray, iron-black
HARDNESS	6-6.5
ENVIRONMENT	Hydrothermal replacement deposits, sediments, epithermal veins
OCCURRENCES	Africa, Czechoslovakia, England, India, Italy, Mexico, Russia; Arkansas, Georgia, Michigan, Minnesota, New Mexico, USA
VALUE	$15+ per specimen

Metaphysical Properties

Pyrolusite is a mineral of transformation that provides positive changes within the user's life on a basic level, such as increasing confidence and optimism. Force fields may also be emitted from pyrolusite to ward off psychic attacks from people who wish the user harm or negative feelings.

Pyromorphite

ASTROLOGICAL SIGN

Sagittarius

Aries

Leo

VIBRATES TO THE NUMBER

7

Unusual pyromorphite crystal cluster from the Daoping Mine, China, cabinet specimen.
Photo courtesy of Mike Keim.

RULES

Solar Plexus

Heart

Pyromorphite is lead chlorophosphate and forms as small, stubby, barrel-shaped, prismatic crystals, often hollow; also as parallel aggregates, reniform masses and crusts. Pyromorphite is translucent with a resinous to adamantine luster. Pyromorphite is an ore of lead and part of a series with two other minerals, mimetite and vanadinite. The resemblance in chemical character is so close between the minerals that, as a rule, it is only possible to distinguish between them by chemical tests. Pyromorphite is often associated with barite and vanadinite and is a popular mineral specimen among mineral collectors.

SYSTEM	Hexagonal
COLOR	Green, yellow-green, white, brown, gray, colorless
HARDNESS	3.5-4
ENVIRONMENT	Oxidation zone of lead deposits
OCCURRENCES	Australia, Canada, China, Czechoslovakia, Germany, Mexico; Idaho, Pennsylvania, USA
VALUE	$30+ per specimen

Metaphysical Properties

Pyromorphite stimulates energy from within the user to provide innovative ways to carry out mundane tasks with a freshness and newness of mind. Pyromorphite also repels negative energies or psychic interference from others and assists other healing stones to bring forth their innate abilities when used together.

Quartz

Quartz is silicon dioxide and commonly forms as well-developed, prismatic, hexagonal crystals, frequently twinned, commonly with some horizontal striation on prism faces; sometimes double-terminated; usually in aggregate groups or clusters; also as fine druses, granular, and massive. Quartz crystals frequently form the inner lining of geodes. Most geodes have an inner layer of larger crystalline quartz, and an outer layer of chalcedony or banded agate. Quartz crystals vary greatly in shape and size and are often uniquely identifiable with their pointed and often uneven terminations. Quartz is transparent to opaque depending on the amount of mineral impurities, and has a vitreous to waxy luster. Quartz is one of the most well known minerals on earth. It occurs in basically all mineral environments, and is the important constituent of many rocks. Quartz is also one of the most varied of all minerals, occurring in numerous different forms, habits, and colors. There are more variety names given to quartz than any other mineral. And, although the feldspars as a group are more prevalent than quartz, as an individual mineral, quartz is the most common.

The two main classifications of the quartz crystal structure are the *macrocrystalline* type and the *cryptocrystalline* type. The cryptocrystalline type, which is defined as having a crystalline structure so fine that no distinct crystals are recognizable under a microscope, is the type of quartz that is the basis for the more massive, solid forms of rock that include the chalcedonies, agates, and jaspers.

The macrocrystalline type of quartz is defined as a solid material whose constituents, such as atoms, molecules or ions, are arranged in a highly ordered microscopic structure, forming individual crystals that are visible to the naked eye. It is the macrocrystalline form of quartz that we will be concerned with here.

In metaphysical practice, all quartz crystals have 6 primary properties. They are able to structure, store, amplify, focus, transmit and transform energy, which includes matter, thought, emotion and information. Metaphysical quartz formations possess special properties based on their geometry, numeric vibrations, crystal structure, mineral inclusions, point of origin, and other specific features.

Due to the fact that there is such a wide array of quartz varieties (with new forms and spiritual properties continually being discovered), we have broken them down into groups according to their crystal form, color, and type of inclusions. Each form, color, and type of inclusion has its own special characteristics that it imparts to the crystals. All of the crystals in this section have the basic traits of clear quartz, or *rock crystal*, and the additional qualities augment and expand on the core values of the pure, colorless crystals. Since quartz crystals are some of the most popular stones used in spiritual healing practices, their metaphysical properties will be a primary focus here.

Amethyst crystals in quartz matrix pocket from Jacksons Crossroads, Georgia, USA, cabinet. Photo courtesy of Larry Michon collection.

Quartz Varieties According to Color

Amethyst Quartz: Purple, colored by ferric iron. Sometimes included with a translucent, white v-shaped pattern called *chevron*. Amethyst is a stone of contentment and spirituality that facilitates the movement of lower energies to the higher frequencies, creating a complete metamorphosis within the individual. Amethyst helps guard against psychic attacks and aids in clearing the aura of any dysfunctional conditions.

Ametrine Quartz: Purple (amethyst) and yellow (citrine) combined. Ametrine is a combination of amethyst and citrine, embracing the qualities of both. Ametrine also enhances spiritual equilibrium and connects one to a more complete state of perfection.

Aura Quartz: A type of color-plated crystals with man-made, iridescent colors created by processes where the crystals are heated and combinations of fine vaporized minerals such as gold, platinum, silver, nickel, iron oxide, cobalt, niobium, or indium are bonded to the crystal surfaces.

Varieties of Aura Quartz Include:

Angel Aura (light blue, silvery, colored by platinum and silver): Meditating with this crystal allows one to enter a state of serenity, peace, purification and rest, and to go beyond the body to perceive and receive help from one's angel guides. It may be used to align and purify all chakras.

Apple Aura (yellow-green, colored by nickel): The Apple Aura crystal is a protector of the spleen, the organ responsible for purifying the blood and boosting the immune system. Worn over the base of the sternum or taped over the spleen chakra, it fights energy drains and overcomes psychic vampirism.

Aqua Aura (aquamarine, colored by gold): It has a calm, relaxing effect on the emotional body and is exceptional for releasing negativity and stress, soothing and healing the aura. It is particularly stimulating to the throat chakra, enhancing one's ability to express emotions in a constructive and positive manner.

Champagne Aura (smoky-golden, colored by gold, indium and iron oxide): A high vibrational crystal of transmutation and spiritual harmony, helping one to ground energetic and psychological changes into the body and to put one's spiritual ideals into practice. Champagne Aura stimulates the sacral and solar plexus chakras, and is an excellent talisman for those new to spiritual work.

Cobalt Aura (deep blue, colored by cobalt): It is an excellent aid to creativity and also increases one's natural clairvoyance and healing powers. Cobalt Aura is stimulating to the throat chakra and removes the constraints of self-expression that may hold one back in life, relationships, or the workplace.

Flame Aura (blue-violet-gold, colored by titanium and niobium): Excellent for use in spiritual initiations and rituals, and for deepening meditation and spiritual attunement. Stimulates the third eye and higher crown chakras.

Amethyst Quartz

Parent amethyst crystal with child from Brazil, large cabinet.
Photo courtesy of Patti Polk; Barbara Grill collection.

Ametrine Quartz

Ametrine crystal from Bolivia, miniature.
Photo courtesy of Amir Chossrow Akhavan collection.

Opal Aura (pearly rainbow colors, colored by platinum): Opal Aura has an intense, strong energy that cleanses the aura, and stimulates, balances, and clears all chakras. It is also a crystal of joy, and like a rainbow, signifies hope and optimism.

Rainbow Aura (vivid multiple colors, colored by gold and titanium): Rainbow Aura activates all the energy centers in the body, clearing a path for the life force to manifest throughout the subtle bodies, bringing in a vibrant energy and zest for life.

Rose Aura (rose, raspberry, colored by platinum and gold or silver): The gentle energy of Rose Aura is uplifting but not overwhelming, and produces a marvelous frequency that stimulates the pineal gland and the heart chakra to transmute deeply held doubts about self-worth.

Ruby Aura (ruby red, colored by platinum and gold or silver): A favorite among women, Ruby Aura brings in love, passion, and vitality, and activates wisdom of the heart while cleansing the base chakra of old survival issues.

Sunshine Aura (bright yellow, colored by gold and platinum): Sunshine Aura's energy is extremely active, wonderful for stimulating and cleansing the solar plexus chakra. It heals old hurts and traumas, and overcomes a sense of disappointment with life, or bitterness at the lack of opportunities.

Tangerine Aura (yellow-orange, colored by gold and iron oxide): Tangerine Aura unites the base, sacral, and solar plexus chakras to provide a cleansing, energetic flow throughout the body and to stimulate one's creativity.

Tanzine Aura (blue-violet, colored by gold, indium and niobium): It opens and aligns the highest crown chakras, and offers deep spiritual comfort, dissolving emotional blockages and replacing them with unconditional love and the sense of being part of a greater soul group.

Blue Quartz: Blue, usually colored by inclusions of riebeckite, dumortierite, or tourmaline. Very rare. Blue quartz inspires hope, aids in healing the soul, and removes fearful blockages when reaching out to others.

Citrine Quartz: Yellow to brownish-yellow, colored by colloidal iron hydrates, and occasionally by aluminum. Citrine dissipates and transmutes any accumulated negative energies within both the physical and subtle bodies, and also is known as a stone that assists in creating and maintaining wealth. Due to their ability to resist negativity, citrine crystals never need cleansing or clearing.

Ferruginous Quartz: Red, colored by inclusions of iron compounds, usually iron oxides (hematite). True red quartz is rare. Red quartz supports the vitality and energy of the physical body and strengthens the nervous system.

Aura Quartz

Tanzine aura quartz cluster from Mexico, small cabinet.
Photo courtesy of Patti Polk; Barbara Grill collection.

Blue Quartz

Blue quartz crystal from Brazil, miniature.
Photo courtesy of Amir Chossrow Akhavan collection.

Ferruginous Quartz: Orange, colored by inclusions of iron compounds, usually iron oxides (hematite). Another variety of orange quartz called *tangerine* is coated externally with iron oxides, causing it to appear orange, but the crystal itself is colorless. Orange quartz also supports the vitality of the physical body while also assisting in creating an optimistic and cheerful emotional attitude.

Milky Quartz: Cloudy white, opaque, generally colored by minute bubbles of gas or liquids trapped within the crystal during formation, and usually massive. Milky quartz aids in letting go of the feelings of being overburdened by one's responsibilities and assists the user to break free of limiting behaviors or feelings of victimization.

Pink Quartz: Pink, colored by aluminum and phosphorus. Not to be confused with rose quartz, which is colored by other minerals. True pink quartz is quite rare. Pink quartz is a crystal of kindness and matters of the heart, much the same as rose quartz. Pink quartz also adds a softening quality to the emotional state and aids the user in finding emotional balance within themselves and compassion for other people who need comforting.

Prasiolite Quartz: Green, colored by trace amounts of naturally irradiated iron. Prasiolite quartz is a stabilizing stone that enhances the strength of the physical body and provides for healing of the heart and aids in allowing the user to practice forgiveness for others.

Rock Crystal Quartz: Colorless, clear. Clear quartz crystal is the universal stone. It corresponds to all zodiac signs, is a tonic for all chakras, and is a pure and powerful energy source. It receives, activates, stores, transmits, and amplifies energy. Stimulates brain functions and activates all levels of consciousness. Excellent for meditation and brings harmony to the soul.

Rose Quartz: A pinkish-rose color that is colored by manganese or titanium. Rose quartz is generally massive and will very rarely form in individual crystals. Rose quartz is the ultimate stone for dealing with all matters of the heart, including self-love and love for others. Rose quartz brings calmness to the heart and peacefulness to personal relationships. Rose quartz aids in healing emotional wounds and promotes a loving nature within the individual.

Smoky Quartz: Brown to brownish-black, colored by traces of aluminum and by natural radioactivity within the earth. Smoky quartz aids in one's ability to dissolve negative energy and to remove emotional blockages within the user. Smoky quartz is also an excellent grounding stone and a powerful protector from outside negative influences that would harm the individual.

Red quartz crystal from Spain, miniature. Photo courtesy of Amir Chossrow Akhavan collection.

Citrine Quartz

Citrine crystal from Russia, miniature.
Photo courtesy of Amir Chossrow Akhavan collection.

Ferruginous Quartz

Orange quartz crystal
from Africa, miniature.
Photo courtesy of Amir Chossrow
Akhavan collection.

Milky Quartz

Milky quartz cluster from
Arizona, small cabinet.
Photo courtesy of Patti Polk collection.

Pink Quartz

Pink quartz crystals
from Brazil, miniature.
Photo courtesy of Amir Chossrow
Akhavan collection.

Prasiolite Quartz

Green prasiolite
crystal cluster from
Greece, miniature.
Photo courtesy of Amir Chossrow
Akhavan collection.

Rock Crystal Quartz

Clear rock crystal quartz point from
Arkansas, USA, small cabinet.
Photo courtesy of Patti Polk collection.

Rose Quartz

Rose quartz cluster from
Brazil, miniature.
Photo courtesy of Dr. Robert Lavinsky collection.

Smoky Quartz

Smoky quartz crystals on petrified wood
from Arizona, USA, large cabinet.
Photo courtesy of Patti Polk collection.

Quartz Varieties According to Form

Barnacle Crystal: A crystal covered or partially covered with smaller crystals. The larger crystal is the "Old Soul" and contains the wisdom and trust that attracts the smaller crystals. Barnacle crystals are used in meditation to provide insights to family and/or community problems. Also excellent for those employed in service organizations to help stimulate a group cohesiveness and willingness to work together.

Bridge or Penetration Crystal: A large crystal with a smaller crystal that penetrates it and is located partially in, and partially out of, the larger crystal. Bridge crystals facilitate the bridging between the inner and outer worlds, between the self and others, and the self and other worlds. Bridge/penetrator crystals also assist one in getting to the root of one's problems by helping one to delve into the activity to which one is determined to move into and removing the blocks to what seems to be too hard to accomplish.

Cactus or Spirit Crystal: Cactus or Spirit quartz is a quartz crystal that is covered with many tiny pointed crystal faces. Cactus quartz is said to clear your aura and all chakras and can remove negative energy or attachments. Cactus quartz elixirs have been used in the treatment of conditions and allergic reactions that are manifested via the skin. Cactus quartz has been used in the treatment of colon disorders, in detoxification of the body and in dealing with obsessive behavior patterns.

Barnacle Crystal

Barnacle crystal from Arkansas, USA, miniature.
Photo courtesy of Patti Polk collection.

Bridge or Penetration Crystal

Bridge quartz crystal from Arkansas, USA, miniature.
Photo courtesy of Patti Polk collection.

Smoky quartz crystal pen-
etrated by a clear quartz
crystal from Payson, Ari-
zona, USA, large cabinet.
Photo courtesy of Patti Polk collection.

Cactus or Spirit Crystal

Light amethyst cactus quartz
cluster from Africa, small cabinet.
Photo courtesy of Larry Michon collection.

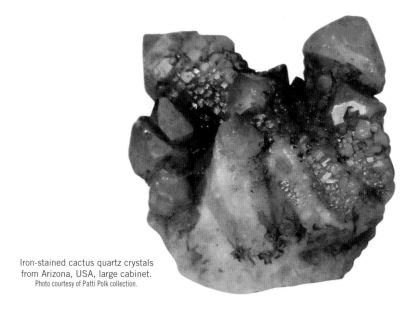

Iron-stained cactus quartz crystals
from Arizona, USA, large cabinet.
Photo courtesy of Patti Polk collection.

Channeling Crystal: Channeling crystals are recognized by a large seven-sided face located in the center front position of the terminated end of the crystal with a triangular face located on the opposite (back) side of the crystal. Channeling crystals provide for a conscious connection to the wisdom that is available from the higher self and to the wisdom of experience and enlightenment which is available from the "other side."

Curved or Bent Crystal: Curved crystals have a curved or bent shape and are a rare occurrence. Curved crystals emanate a gentle yet powerful energy and can be used to cleanse the aura, promote flexibility in one's attitude, and provide strength in decision-making.

Double-Terminated Crystal: These crystals have a point on each opposite end (termination) and are formed independently as a floater instead of growing out from a matrix. They have the capacity to both push and pull energy through their terminations. By placing a double-terminated crystal between the chakras, it can be used to move energy both upwards and downwards through the chakra column of the physical body.

Druse or Druzy Crystal: Druzy crystals are a surface coating of small crystal points that cover a matrix. Druzy crystals are good for people who want to develop new ideas or thought forms and expand their horizons.

Elestial Crystal: Elestial crystals are recognized by multi-terminations on the body and/or faces of a layered and/or etched crystal. Elestial quartz crystals stimulate the actualization of the conscious self. They serve to provide an entrance to information concerning the past, present, and future of one's existence. The elestial crystal contains the absolute and ultimate essential wisdom and can provide for the transfer of insight to the physical intellect via the higher-self and can be used to sustain and maintain equilibrium during stressful periods of change.

Faden Crystal: Faden crystals have one or more milky "feathery" thread lines, usually running edge-to-edge through the length of the crystal and usually perpendicular to the crystals growth. The faden crystal is one of connection and stimulation, and aids in establishing a connective force between the self and that which is one's objective. It is also a stone for the exploration of the parallel dimensions of one's reality. It strengthens the "silver cord" and produces an energy that both promotes and protects one during flight.

Channeling Crystal

Channeling crystal from Brazil, small cabinet. Photo courtesy of Kevin Burgart collection.

Curved or Bent Crystal

Curved, pink Lemurian seed crystal point from Brazil, miniature. Photo courtesy of Patti Polk; Kevin Burgart collection.

Double-Terminated Crystal

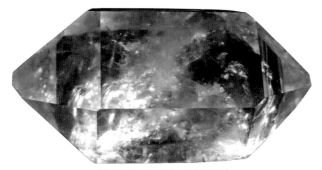

Double-terminated quartz crystal
from Arizona, USA, miniature.
Photo courtesy of Patti Polk collection.

Druse or Druzy Crystal

A small opal aura geode with
internal druzy quartz crystals
from Brazil, small cabinet.
Photo courtesy of Patti Polk collection.

A carpet of fine druzy quartz crystals over
agate from Montana, USA, small cabinet.
Photo courtesy of Patti Polk collection.

Elestial Crystal

Elestial crystal from Brazil,
small cabinet.
Photo courtesy of Kevin Burgart collection.

Faden Crystal

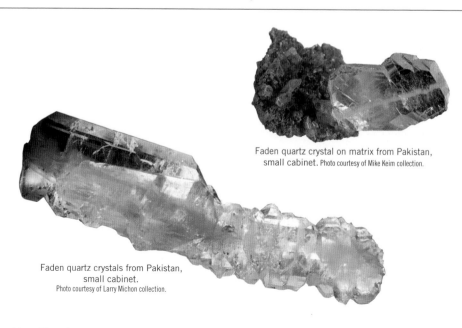

Faden quartz crystal on matrix from Pakistan,
small cabinet. Photo courtesy of Mike Keim collection.

Faden quartz crystals from Pakistan,
small cabinet.
Photo courtesy of Larry Michon collection.

Geode Crystals: Geode crystals are quartz crystals that form inside the walls of a geode. They are attached to the rock walls and are pointing inward toward the center of the void. Geode crystals prompt us to look within to find our own personal truths. Geode crystals also provide a safe haven for weary travelers and bring healing to anyone located within their vicinity.

Generator Crystal: A generator crystal is a quartz crystal point in which the terminating point derives from six equant sides. Natural generator quartz points are relatively rare, although cut and polished points are readily available that have similar properties. Generator crystals are powerful magnifiers of energy, and are important as a tool for healing practitioners. Generator quartz facilitates the cleansing and balancing of the chakras, and focuses healing intentions for individuals, groups, and the Earth.

Key Crystal: The key crystal recognized by a three- or six-sided indented crystal shape located on the face of a crystal. The indent becomes narrower as it goes within the crystal, and ends within the crystal, usually in an apex termination. It is used to unlock the doors to healing concepts and to expose those aspects of the self that tend to be hidden from view.

Laser Wand Crystal: Laser wand crystals are recognized as long slender crystals with small faces that meet at the termination. The available energy of the laser wand crystal is extremely well focused through the small termination and is often used to clear an area of negative energy. Laser wands are also excellent protective barriers when held near the physical body.

Lemurian Seed Crystal: These unique crystals are clear quartz but can often have a tinge of pink, and instead of having a shiny surface, they may appear frosted or dull, like they have a matte finish. Their most unique characteristic is a series of horizontal striations that run up one or more of the sides of the crystal. Usually, these distinct horizontal striations end in a triangular face, forming the apex of the crystal. Lemurian seed crystals are reputed to have been left to us by the Lemurians, an advanced ancient civilization, to teach and guide us in this time. Lemurians hold and transmit messages of unconditional love, equality, and spiritual teachings. Lemurian seed crystals have a feminine energy, and for all their power, are more energetically gentle than masculine crystals. Lemurians are very powerful tools for meditation, clearing and balancing all chakras, and for healing on all levels.

Manifestation Crystal: The manifestation crystal is a small crystal totally enclosed within a larger crystal. These crystals are quite rare and one must clear any feelings of ambivalence and inner turmoil prior to using them. These crystals can be used to facilitate artistic creativity, creative thinking, and to increase or decrease any aspect of one's life.

Geode Crystals

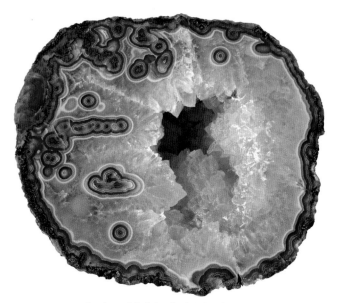

Quartz crystals lining the interior of an agate geode
from Mexico, large cabinet.
Photo courtesy of Patti Polk; Klaus Klement collection.

Generator Crystal

Polished generator crystal with inclusions from Brazil, small cabinet.
Photo courtesy of Patti Polk collection.

Key Crystal

A self-healed key crystal
with barnacles from
Arkansas, USA, miniature.
Photo courtesy of Patti Polk collection.

Laser Wand Crystal

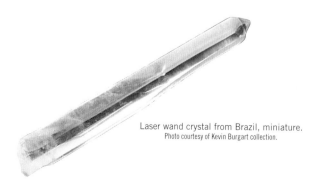

Laser wand crystal from Brazil, miniature.
Photo courtesy of Kevin Burgart collection.

Lemurian Seed Crystal

Amethyst Lemurian seed
crystal point from New
Mexico, USA, miniature.
Photo courtesy of Patti Polk; Kevin
Kessler collection.

Manifestation Crystal

Twinned manifestation crystal
with completely included quartz
crystals and a window from Herkimer, New York, USA, thumbnail.
Photo courtesy of Patti Polk collection.

Manifestation crystal with included
quartz crystal from Brazil, miniature.
Photo courtesy of Patti Polk collection.

Phantom Crystal: Phantom crystals are crystals that exhibit a secondary ghost-like image or "phantom" of another crystal seated within the main crystal. The phantoms are created by patterns of particles of various minerals that were included during an interruption in the crystal's growth. Phantom crystals are used for the redemption and cleansing of the earth. The phantom works to bring together the participants of humanity to heal the planet and can also be used to access the records of one's progression through past lives.

Rainbow Crystal: A crystal with internal fracturing that causes colorful prismatic rainbows inside the crystal when viewed in the proper light. Rainbow crystals promote hope, happiness, and optimism and awaken us to the beauty in nature.

Record Keeper or Recorder Crystal: A Record Keeper, or Recorder, crystal is one that has pyramidal or triangular-shaped figures that are either engraved into, or are raised on, one or more of a crystal's faces. These symbols are not always obvious and usually need to be seen by looking closely at the crystal surface faces in a bright light. It is believed that the record keeper is one of the most sacred crystals because it holds the wisdom and knowledge of the universe. When a person is properly attuned to a record keeper, this knowledge is readily made available.

Scepter Crystal: A scepter quartz crystal is formed when a secondary crystal has grown over and around the end of an existing base crystal. Scepter crystals are essentially masculine in energy and are best suited to positive and assertive actions. An example of where this might be useful would be in a situation where a person would need to assert personal power to accomplish a task. Scepters were believed to have been used in Atlantis and Lemuria in healing ceremonies and were a symbol of the power of the realm, used by people such as a high priest or priestess. Scepters are excellent conductors for transmission of directional energy and believed to enhance fertility.

There is a location in the United States that is noted for exceptionally powerful amethyst scepter quartz crystals known as "Smokey Rose" crystals, located in New Mexico. According to current interpretations, these crystals are more powerful than super seven crystals, encompass all numerical vibrations, and are capable of attaining frequencies of all levels and all dimensions for universal awareness. See Resources for contact information about fee-digging opportunities for Smokey Rose crystals.

Self-Healed Crystal: Self-healed crystals are recognized by crystalline structures appearing regrown where a crystal was previously broken. Having learned to heal itself, these crystals can reveal this knowledge to someone in the process of healing themselves or others. Self-healed quartz crystals are teaching us by example that nothing is ever too late, or too damaged, to be able to reach the state of inherent perfection.

Phantom Crystal

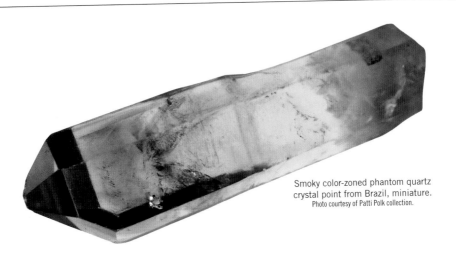

Smoky color-zoned phantom quartz
crystal point from Brazil, miniature.
Photo courtesy of Patti Polk collection.

Rainbow Crystal

Quartz crystal with colorful internal
rainbow from Arizona, USA, miniature.
Photo courtesy of Patti Polk collection.

Record Keeper or Recorder Crystal

Record-keeper crystal from Brazil, miniature. Photo courtesy of Kevin Burgart collection.

Scepter Crystal

Smokey Rose amethyst scepter crystal on matrix from New Mexico, USA, small cabinet. Photo courtesy of Patti Polk; Kevin Kessler collection.

Self-Healed Crystal

Small self-healed amethyst crystal from New Mexico, USA, thumbnail. Photo courtesy of Patti Polk; Kevin Kessler collection.

Skeletal Crystal: Skeletal quartz crystals are characterized by geometric depressions that produce pronounced external etching and internal cavities that give an overall skeletal appearance. In these crystals, the edges grew more quickly than the faces, so the edges stand out like the frames of a window. Skeletal quartz crystal allows for deeper vision, clairvoyance, and access to the inner working of spirit, mind, and emotional states. It is an excellent stone for the shaman and mystic, who may utilize its properties for soul-journeys. Skeletal crystals also possess the properties of the elestial crystal formation.

Tabby Crystal: A tabby is a flat crystal, usually with etching or striations on one side with the width being at least twice the thickness of the depth. Tabby crystals can be used to activate other crystals, and to enhance communication, understanding, and dialogue between people and nature.

Transmitter Crystal: A transmitter crystal is recognized by having two larger and relatively symmetrical seven-sided faces on either side of a small triangle. Also known as the seven-three-seven configuration, transmitters are good for long-distance healing and for improving connections to the higher self for the enhancement of personal creative forces.

Trigonic Crystal: Trigonic crystals are some of the rarest formations of the quartz crystal family. Trigonic crystals have an indented, downward-pointed triangle in one or more of the termination faces, similar to a record keeper, except for the downward-pointing direction. Trigonic crystals aid in periods of transition, both physically and astrally, and are protectors of those who visit other worlds to seek access to past and future knowledge.

Twinned Crystal: Twinned crystals are crystals that exhibit a specific type of twinning law structure. The most well-known types of twins are the Japan Law twin and the Dauphine Law twin. Japan Law twins are contact twin crystals where the c-axis of the two crystals are intersected at an 84 degree angle, and Dauphine Law twins are penetration twins intergrown as one crystal and exhibit either a left-handed or right-handed crystal structure that is rotated around the c-axis by 60 degrees relative to each other. There are also crystals that have a parallel growth structure adjacent to each other that appear to be twins, called "soulmate twins," but are not actually true twins. Twinned crystals are used to dissipate and transmute deviations, working out problems on both the physical and subtle levels. Twinned crystals are excellent for clearing the aura and for aligning the auric body with the physical structure. Twins also help to stabilize emotions, dispel anger, and encourage one to achieve harmony and balance with others.

Window Crystal: Window crystals exhibit a diamond-shaped window surface that is formed where the sides and faces of a crystal intersect. Window crystals are primarily used for "seeing" within ourselves to further our personal spiritual development. Many forms of divination can be enhanced by the use of these crystals and window crystals can be particularly helpful in revealing the state of health or dis-ease within others when requested to do so.

Skeletal Crystal

Smokey Rose skeletal amethyst quartz crystal from
Brushy Mountain Mine, New Mexico, USA, miniature.
Photo courtesy of Patti Polk; Kevin Kessler collection.

Tabby Crystal

Tabby quartz crystal from Arkansas,
USA, small cabinet.
Photo courtesy of Patti Polk; Barbara Grill collection.

Transmitter Crystal

Colorless transmitter crystal from Brazil,
miniature. Photo courtesy of Kevin Burgart collection.

Trigonic Crystal

Trigonic crystal from Brazil, miniature.
Photo courtesy of Kevin Burgart collection.

Twinned Crystal

Clear quartz crystals twinned in the Japan Law habit from Peru, small cabinet.
Photo courtesy of Patti Polk collection.

Clear quartz "soulmate" crystals, a type of parallel growth pattern, from Brazil, small cabinet.
Photo courtesy of Patti Polk collection.

Window Crystal

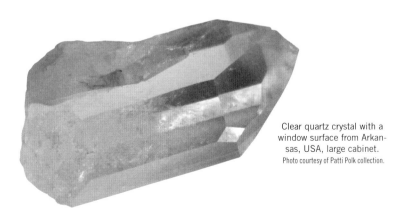

Clear quartz crystal with a window surface from Arkansas, USA, large cabinet.
Photo courtesy of Patti Polk collection.

Quartz

Quartz Varieties According to Inclusions

Aventurine: A massive green granular cryptocrystalline quartz with platelike crystals of mica that gives it a sparkly, shimmering effect. Not a macrocrystalline form, but included here due to its use as a healing stone. Aventurine helps to balance the masculine and feminine energies, enhances creativity, and strengthens the spirit in new endeavors. Also, useful in shielding the heart from unwanted intrusions.

Dendritic Quartz: Quartz crystal exhibiting brown or black dendritic, flowering patterns due to the inclusion of manganese. Dendritic quartz is a crystal of bonding, bringing others closer, and activating the energies of cooperation in group efforts. Dendritic quartz also produces a grounding effect that helps to balance the emotions with the physical body.

Dumortierite Quartz: Quartz crystal containing fine blue radiating sprays of the mineral dumortierite. Dumortierite quartz enhances all mental abilities and assists in making difficult decisions and dealing with apparently hopeless situations. Dumortierite quartz helps to access the information needed from the higher self to guide one's self or others in moving forward on their path and to clear blockages in the chakra system.

Enhydro Quartz: A quartz crystal containing an internal, sealed pocket of water, often showing a visible moving air bubble trapped inside. The enhydro assists in compassionate understanding of the feelings of others, and also provides for concentrated determination in the effort of self-transformation.

Metallic Included Quartz: Quartz crystal containing metallic inclusions, such as gold, copper, pyrite, and other metals. Metallic included quartz amplifies the character of whichever metal is included in the quartz crystal.

> **Gold:** Gold helps to balance the energy fields and dispels feeling of inferiority. Gold also may aid in attracting honor and prosperity.

> **Copper:** Copper stimulates optimism, diplomacy, and independence, and may be considered "lucky" and helpful in the recovery of lost items.

> **Pyrite:** Pyrite works as a shield against negative energies and helps to promote the nourishing energies of the body.

Mineral Included Quartz: Quartz crystal containing mineral inclusions, such as carbon, chlorite, fluorite, goethite, hematite, lithium, hedenbergite, and others. For example, hematite-included quartz contains both the amplification properties of quartz with the balance and stability of hematite and assists in balancing the body, mind, and spirit, whereas chlorite included quartz focuses on purifying and detoxifying the physical and auric bodies.

Aventurine

Massive aventurine from India, small cabinet.
Photo courtesy of Patti Polk collection.

Dendritic Quartz

Faceted quartz crystal with included
dendrites from Brazil, small cabinet.
Photo courtesy of Larry Michon collection.

Dumortierite Quartz

Quartz crystal with dumortierite inclusions from Brazil, thumbnail.
Photo courtesy of Yoshihiro Kobayashi collection.

Enhydro Quartz

Enhydro quartz showing a visible air bubble
inside the water-included crystal, from Brazil,
miniature. Photo courtesy of Patti Polk collection.

Metallic Included Quartz

Clear crystal point pendant with included
pyrite flakes from Arizona, USA, miniature.
Photo courtesy of Patti Polk collection.

Mineral Included Quartz

Known as "Fire" or "Harlequin"
quartz, a crystal with hematite inclusions from Brazil, small cabinet.
Photo courtesy of Patti Polk collection.

Quartz crystal point with
chlorite inclusions from
Brazil, small cabinet.
Photo courtesy of Patti Polk;
Barbara Grill collection.

Oil Included Quartz: Unusual quartz crystals from Pakistan that contain small pockets of yellow-colored, natural petroleum oil. Oil is the condensed solar energy of ancient organic matter and this is the signature of these crystals. Each one contains a tiny but potent spark of solar energy, perfectly preserved and amplified by the quartz. The beautiful golden-yellow colors in these crystals give a special resonance with the solar plexus chakra, helping to engender cheerfulness and emotional optimism.

Rutilated Quartz: Quartz crystal containing acicular needles of red, gold or brown rutile. Rutilated quartz assists one in the understanding and solving of personal problems, and provides awareness of the connections between the physical and astral planes during astral travel.

Star or Spider Quartz: Quartz crystal containing the mineral hollandite that forms patterns like tiny black stars or spiders floating in the crystal. Black star crystals rule the crown chakra and help to develop psychic vision while also encouraging powerful coincidental or synchronistic events to manifest in your life.

Super Seven Quartz: Super Seven crystals, also known as Melody Stones or Sacred Seven, are a combination of amethyst quartz, clear quartz, and smoky quartz, included with the minerals cacoxenite, goethite, lepidocrocite, and rutile that come specifically from Brazil. Super Seven is a rather interesting crystal due to the fact that it is one of the few stones that retains all the energy, purpose, and clarity of each mineral individually, yet each are able to work together in unity. It is a powerful stone for healing the earth, mind, body, and spiritual diseases. The very nature of the stone means that it is not associated with any one chakra, instead it is distinguished by its ability to heal, balance, and energize all seven chakras, hence the name Super Seven. A close relative, auralite 23 comes from Canada and contains 23 different minerals including titanite, cacoxenite, lepidocrocite, ajoite, hematite, magnetite, pyrite, goethite, pyrolusite, gold, silver, platinum, nickel, copper, iron, limonite, sphalerite, covellite, chalcopyrite, gialite, epidote, bornite, and rutile.

Super Seven crystals support spiritual development, dispel negative energy, and heal on all levels. Super Seven crystals are highly prized for their ability to awaken many types of psychic abilities, such as the ability to see auras, telepathy, clairvoyance, clairaudience, channeling, and telekinesis.

Tibetan Quartz: Quartz crystals from Nepal that contain fragments of chlorite, and also exhibit fine external chlorite coatings. Real Nepalese crystals are relatively rare and are prized for their uniquely mystical vibration. Tibetan quartz enhances meditation and yoga practices as well as initiating and strengthening all the subtle faculties, and are appropriate for healing all chakra centers.

Tourmalinated Quartz: Quartz crystal containing crystals of tourmaline, usually schorl (black), sometimes indicolite. Tourmalinated quartz helps to eliminate destructive habitual patterns in one's life and is an excellent protector against any negative external influences.

Oil Included Quartz

Clear, double-terminated quartz crystal with
oil inclusion cluster from Pakistan, thumbnail.
Photo courtesy of Patti Polk collection.

Rutilated Quartz

Rutilated quartz crystal cluster from Brazil, small cabinet.
Photo courtesy of Dr. Robert Lavinsky collection.

Star or Spider Quartz

"Spider" or "Black Star" quartz crystal included with
hollandite crystals from Madagascar, thumbnail.
Photo courtesy of Stacie Hirsch Nutter collection.

Super Seven Quartz

Super seven crystal from
Brazil, miniature.
Photo courtesy of Patti Polk collection.

Tibetan Quartz

Tibetan quartz cluster with chlorite inclusions
and coatings from Nepal, small cabinet.
Photo courtesy of Patti Polk; Kevin Burgart collection.

Tourmalinated Quartz

Tourmalinated quartz crystal from Brazil, small cabinet.
Photo courtesy of Patti Polk collection.

Some forms of quartz, especially the semi-precious stones that are used in jewelry making, commonly have their color enhanced. Almost all forms of the yellow-golden variety of citrine are heat-treated, as well as amethyst to intensify its purple color. A green transparent form, known as "Green Amethyst" or "Prasiolite" is also created by heat-treating certain types of amethyst, although genuine prasiolite does rarely occur naturally.

There are also some varieties of quartz crystals that are known for their specific locations such as the famous Herkimer "Diamonds" from Herkimer, New York; Payson "Diamonds" from Arizona; Pecos "Diamonds" from New Mexico; the distinctive individual and crystal clusters from the Ouachita district in Arkansas; the iron-encrusted amethyst specimens from Thunder Bay, Canada; the excellent hedenbergite included crystals from Mongolia; and the unique, lustrous crystals from Brandburg, Namibia, Africa.

SYSTEM	Hexagonal
COLOR	Colorless, white, yellow, pink, red, orange, purple, green, blue, brown to black
HARDNESS	7
ENVIRONMENT	Metamorphic rocks, pegmatites, volcanic rocks, sedimentary rocks
OCCURRENCES	Australia, Africa, Brazil, Canada, Italy, Madagascar, Mexico, Tibet; Arkansas, Arizona, California, Colorado, Maine, New Mexico, New York, US
VALUE	$5+ per specimen

Realgar

ASTROLOGICAL SIGN

Scorpio

RULES

Root

VIBRATES TO THE NUMBER

8

Realgar crystals on matrix from Nevada, cabinet.
Photo courtesy of Patti Polk; Dick Moore collection.

Realgar is arsenic sulfide and forms rarely as small, stubby, prismatic crystals, and more commonly as granular or compact aggregates and earthy crusts. Realgar is also known as "Ruby Sulfur" and is translucent to transparent and has an adamantine luster. Realgar most commonly forms as a low-temperature hydrothermal vein mineral associated with other arsenic and antimony minerals. It also occurs as volcanic sublimations and in hot spring deposits and occurs in association with orpiment, arsenolite, calcite and barite and in the geyser deposits of Yellowstone National Park. Realgar is toxic, and realgar, orpiment, and arsenopyrite provide nearly all the world's supply of arsenic as a byproduct of smelting concentrates derived from these ores. Realgar has also been used in Chinese medicine, as an ingredient in the manufacture of fireworks, and as a paint pigment.

Realgar and orpiment cluster
from Nevada, cabinet.
Photo courtesy of Patti Polk; Dick Moore collection.

Metaphysical Properties

Realgar brings forth hidden memories and ideas that are buried within the user's subconscious so that they can be utilized and examined within the physical plane. Upon reflection of revealed things, acceptance may be obtained with this mineral, and effective progression toward genuine contentment may be achieved.

SYSTEM	Monoclinic
COLOR	Deep red-orange
HARDNESS	1.5-2
ENVIRONMENT	Low temperature hydrothermal veins, hot springs
OCCURRENCES	China, Hungary, Italy, Peru, Romania, Spain, Switzerland; California, Nevada, Utah, Washington, USA
VALUE	$40+ per specimen

Rhodochrosite

ASTROLOGICAL SIGN

Scorpio

♌

Leo

RULES

Solar Plexus

Heart

VIBRATES TO THE NUMBER

4

Rhodochrosite crystals on quartz from the Chacua Mine, Peru, small cabinet. Photo courtesy of Patti Polk; Kevin Kessler collection.

Rhodochrosite is a carbonate of manganese and forms as rhombohedral or scalenohedral crystals, or as stalactitic, mammillary, reniform, or concretionary masses. Rhodochrosite is translucent with a vitreous to pearly luster. Rhodochrosite is mainly used as an ore of manganese, which is a key component of low-cost stainless steel formulations and certain aluminium alloys. Colorful, multi-banded massive pieces are often polished and used as ornamental stones and transparent crystals are cut and faceted as semi-precious gemstones for use in jewelry. Due to their rarity and beauty, fine rhodochrosite crystal specimens are in high demand with crystal collectors.

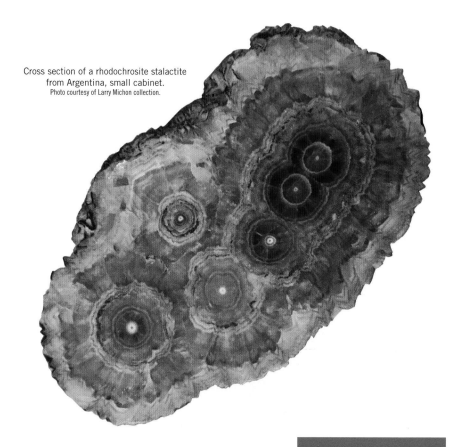

Cross section of a rhodochrosite stalactite
from Argentina, small cabinet.
Photo courtesy of Larry Michon collection.

Metaphysical Properties

Rhodochrosite guides the user's mentality away from thinking in rigid, outdated terms to a new understanding that there is more than just one way of solving problems. Rhodochrosite also aids the user in ceasing to making excuses, or denying change, all the while learning to graciously accept those changes that are necessary to their growth.

SYSTEM	Hexagonal
COLOR	Pink, rose-pink
HARDNESS	3.5-4.5
ENVIRONMENT	Hydrothermal veins
OCCURRENCES	Africa, Argentina, Romania, Spain; Arkansas, Colorado, Montana, USA
VALUE	$50+ per specimen

Rutile

ASTROLOGICAL SIGN

♊
Gemini

♉
Taurus

Venus

VIBRATES TO THE NUMBER

4

RULES

All
Chakras

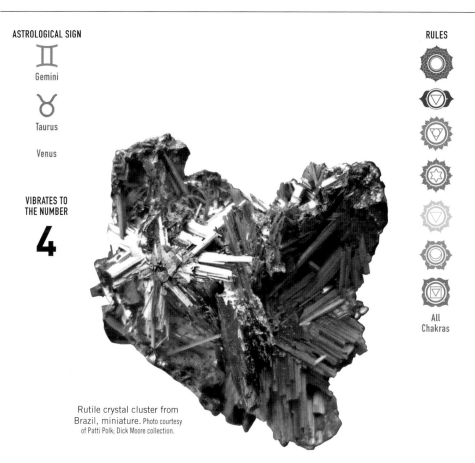

Rutile crystal cluster from Brazil, miniature. Photo courtesy of Patti Polk; Dick Moore collection.

Rutile is titanium dioxide and forms as elongated, prismatic crystals, often striated; also as twins, acicular, and disseminated. Rutile is semi-opaque to translucent with a metallic to adamantine luster. Rutile often occurs as an inclusion in other minerals, such as quartz, where it is known as "Maiden Hair," or more commonly as "Rutilated Quartz." Natural rutile may contain up to 10 percent iron and significant amounts of niobium and tantalum. Rutile has among the highest refractive indices at visible wavelengths of any known crystal, and also exhibits a particularly large birefringence and high dispersion. Owing to these properties, it is useful for the manufacture of certain optical elements, especially polarization optics. Rutile crystals make beautiful display specimens.

R

Terminated, twinned rutile crystal
group from Brazil, miniature.
Photo courtesy of Mike Keim collection.

Rutile crystal from Graves Mountain,
Georgia, USA, miniature.
Photo courtesy of Patti Polk; Kevin Kessler collection.

SYSTEM	Tetragonal
COLOR	Yellow, red, brownish-red, black
HARDNESS	6-6.5
ENVIRONMENT	Plutonic and metamorphic rocks, pegmatites, quartz veins
OCCURRENCES	Australia, Brazil, Mexico, Norway Switzerland; Arkansas, California, Georgia, Virginia, USA
VALUE	$40+ per specimen

Metaphysical Properties

Rutile crystals ward off
harmful interference in both
the physical and spiritual
realms by transmitting
the user's desire to be
left in peace on those
planes. Rutile may also
act as a stabilizer for the
user's mental state when
involving relationships and
imbalances in both mind
and body.

Scheelite

ASTROLOGICAL SIGN

♎︎
Libra

VIBRATES TO THE NUMBER

5

RULES

Crown

Root

Scheelite crystals on matrix from China, small cabinet.
Photo courtesy of Patti Polk; Dick Moore collection.

Scheelite is calcium tungstate and forms as dipyramidal, pseudo-octahedral crystals; sometimes tabular or columnar, and striated on some faces. Scheelite is translucent to transparent with a vitreous to adamantine luster and is an important ore of tungsten. Scheelite fluoresces a bright sky-blue under shortwave UV light, and the presence of molybdenum trace impurities occasionally results in a green glow. The fluorescence of scheelite, sometimes associated with native gold, is sometimes used by geologists in the search for gold deposits. Well-formed crystals are sought by collectors and are occasionally fashioned into gemstones when suitably free of flaws. Scheelite has been synthesized and the material produced may be used to imitate diamond, due to its high refractive index and luster.

SYSTEM	Tetragonal
COLOR	Colorless, white, gray, yellow, orange, green, brown, gray
HARDNESS	4.5-5
ENVIRONMENT	Contact metamorphics, quartz veins, pegmatites
OCCURRENCES	Brazil, Canada, Italy, Korea, Switzerland; Arizona, California, Connecticut, Idaho, USA
VALUE	$20+ per specimen

Metaphysical Properties

Scheelite is used as a spiritual aid during meditation that allows for a sense of peace to be gathered from within the crystal. Scheelite gives the user greater objectivity when dealing with people and their motivations, plus the ability to discern the entire situation as opposed to seeing it from a single point of view.

Scolecite

ASTROLOGICAL SIGN

♑

Capricorn

**VIBRATES TO
THE NUMBER**

1

RULES

Third Eye

Crown

Scolecite crystal cluster
from India, large cabinet
specimen. Photo courtesy of Patti
Polk; Dick Moore collection.

Scolecite is hydrous calcium aluminum silicate and commonly occurs as sprays of thin, prismatic needles, frequently flattened on one side, with slanted terminations and striated parallel to the length of the needles. The crystals appear to be pseudo-orthorhombic or pseudo-tetragonal, and may be square in cross section. It also occurs as radiating groups and fibrous masses. Scolecite is transparent to translucent, has a vitreous to silky luster, and is a member of the zeolite group. Scolecite is pyroelectric and piezoelectric, sometimes fluoresces yellow to brown in longwave and shortwave UV light. Scolecite is primarily used as a display specimen and is highly regarded as a metaphysical stone.

SYSTEM	Monoclinic
COLOR	Colorless, white, pinkish, reddish, greenish
HARDNESS	5-5.5
ENVIRONMENT	Cavities in basalts
OCCURRENCES	Brazil, Iceland, India, Italy, Scotland; Colorado, Georgia, New Jersey, Utah, Washington, USA
VALUE	$40+ per specimen

Metaphysical Properties

Scolecite has the power to bestow inner peace, giving the user the ability to sleep more soundly, experience lucid dreams, and find greater depth in meditation. Scolecite also may bring forth knowledge from both the user's past and future to assist in making decisions while in the present physical plane.

Selenite

ASTROLOGICAL SIGN

♉

Taurus

RULES

Third Eye

Crown

VIBRATES TO THE NUMBER

8

Selenite crystal cluster from Oklahoma, USA, cabinet specimen.
Photo courtesy of Patti Polk collection.

Yellow, transparent selenite crystals from Manitoba, Canada, small cabinet.
Photo courtesy of Mike Keim.

Selenite is a form of gypsum, hydrous calcium sulfate (see Gypsum). Selenite is usually an elongated, transparent, and colorless cleavage section of gypsum. Some selenite may be fluorescent or phosphorescent, and may also feel warm to the touch due to its natural thermal insulating properties. Selenite crystals can range in size from small to giant-sized crystals such as those found in the caves of the Naica Mine in Chihuahua, Mexico, where the spectacular crystals have thrived in the cave's rare natural environment for over 500,000 years and have grown up to 33 feet in length. In the USA, the state of Oklahoma is well known for its variety of selenite specimens, most notably the "Hourglass" type that exhibits an interesting brown-colored hourglass shape within the clear crystal. Selenite is popular as a healing stone and is frequently cut into polished wands for use in healing practices.

SYSTEM	Monoclinic
COLOR	Colorless, may be tinted brown, green, yellow, or gray due to impurities
HARDNESS	2
ENVIRONMENT	Sedimentary rocks, clay beds, hydrothermal replacement deposits
OCCURRENCES	Chile, Italy, Mexico, Morocco; Arizona, Kentucky, New Mexico, New York, Ohio, Oklahoma, Utah, USA
VALUE	$5+ per specimen

Metaphysical Properties

Selenite aids in providing clarity of the mind, which grants the user the necessary tools of discernment to find the best solution to an issue. Selenite also generates access to the user's forgotten past lives as well as predicting future lives through understanding of the current lifestyle path.

Siderite

ASTROLOGICAL SIGN

Aquarius

VIBRATES TO THE NUMBER

44

Siderite crystal rhombs on quartz from Harz Mountains, Germany, small cabinet.
Photo courtesy of Mike Keim.

RULES

All Chakras

Siderite is a mineral composed of iron carbonate and forms as rhombohedral crystals with curved, striated faces, sometimes tabular, prismatic, and in saddle-shaped aggregates; also botryoidal, compact, fibrous, and in concretionary masses. Siderite is transparent to translucent with a vitreous to pearly luster and is associated with barite, fluorite, galena in hydrothermal veins, and it also occurs in shales and sandstones, where it sometimes forms concretions, which can encase three-dimensionally preserved fossils. Siderite is an important iron ore mineral and is primarily used as a display specimen, although it can occasionally be faceted as a semi-precious stone if sufficiently transparent.

SYSTEM	Hexagonal
COLOR	Pale yellow, brown, gray, green, red, black
HARDNESS	3.5-4
ENVIRONMENT	Sedimentary formations, ore veins, pegmatites
OCCURRENCES	Austria, Brazil, Canada, England, Greenland, Italy, Scotland; Arizona, Colorado, Connecticut, Pennsylvania, Vermont, USA
VALUE	$10+ per specimen

Metaphysical Properties

Siderite offers comfort, calmness, and patience for those facing difficult and hurtful situations. Even after being wronged or hurt by someone, the user will find that they are less likely to obsess over the offence and persevere after the confrontation.

Silver

Spinel-twinned silver crystal with "herringbone" effect from the New Nevada Mine, Chihuahua, Mexico, miniature. Photo courtesy of Dr. Robert Lavinsky collection.

Silver is a native element and forms rarely as small, cube-shaped or octahedral crystals with stepped faces; more commonly as wire, dendrites, scales, plates, compact masses, and grains. Silver is opaque, ductile, and malleable, with a metallic luster, and possesses the highest electrical conductivity, thermal conductivity, and reflectivity of any metal. Silver has long been valued as a precious metal used in jewelry making, fine tableware, and for ornamentation purposes. More abundant than gold, silver metal has functioned in many historic monetary systems as currency, and today has many industrial uses such as in chemistry, solar panels, water filtration systems, and in electrical contacts and conductors. Silver-plating is a common process to enhance the value of lesser metals, and dilute silver nitrate solutions and other silver compounds are used as an antiseptic added to wound-dressings. Delicate natural silver wire specimens are highly collectible and beautiful.

SYSTEM	Isometric
COLOR	Silver-white, silver-gray, brownish, black (from tarnish)
HARDNESS	2.5-3
ENVIRONMENT	Ore veins
OCCURRENCES	Australia, Bolivia, Canada, Mexico, Norway, Peru; Arizona, Colorado, Michigan, USA
VALUE	$40+ per specimen

Metaphysical Properties

Silver is a mineral that provides eloquence of speech and refinery to one's character by giving the user an air of charm and charisma. Also, during meditation, it provides the traveling spirit a sure-fire connection back to the physical plane. When silver is used as a setting for gemstones it not only attracts and retains the qualities of the stones, but also directs the energy of other minerals to the appropriate location as needed for balancing and healing.

Smithsonite

ASTROLOGICAL SIGN

Pisces

Virgo

**VIBRATES TO
THE NUMBER**

7

RULES

All
Chakras

Mammilary green smithsonite from the Kelly Mine,
New Mexico, USA, thumbnail.
Photo courtesy of Mike Keim.

Smithsonite is zinc carbonate and rarely forms as rhombohedral or scalenohedral crystals with curved faces; more commonly as botryoidal, mammillary, reniform, or stalactitic aggregates, often concretionary. Smithsonite is translucent with a vitreous to greasy luster and generally occurs as a secondary mineral in the weathering or oxidation zone of zinc-bearing ore deposits with hemimorphite, cerussite, malachite and anglesite. Smithsonite occurs in a variety of colors and is a desirable mineral specimen for many collectors. Occasionally smithsonite is polished as an ornamental stone and may also exhibit fluorescence.

Pink smithsonite from the Refugio
Mine, Mexico, cabinet.
Photo courtesy of Joe Budd, Dr. Robert Lavinsky collection.

Metaphysical Properties

Smithsonite provides the user with the ability and mental endurance to command and bridge a situation that might otherwise lead to unnecessary hurt feelings or confrontation. In terms of psychic abilities, smithsonite may also enhance the user's clairvoyance and clairsentience abilities by confirming the results of messages received by these methods.

SYSTEM	Hexagonal
COLOR	White, gray, yellow, blue-green, green, pink, violet, brown
HARDNESS	5.5
ENVIRONMENT	Oxidation zone of sulfide deposits
OCCURRENCES	Africa, Greece, Mexico, Russia, Spain, Turkey; Arkansas, Colorado, New Mexico, USA
VALUE	$25+ per specimen

Sphaerocobaltite

Heart

Crown

Sphaerocobaltite with malachite from Africa, miniature.
Photo courtesy of Patti Polk collection.

Sphaerocobaltite is a cobalt carbonate of the calcite group that rarely forms as rhombohedral or discoidal crystals, and more commonly as encrustations on the surface of the host matrix. Sphaerocobaltite is an uncommon mineral that is transparent to translucent with a vitreous to waxy luster and is associated with erythrite, roselite, and annabergite in cobalt rich deposits. Sphaerocobaltite is a desirable collectible display mineral due to its unusual, vivid pink color.

SYSTEM	Trigonal
COLOR	Hot pink, magenta, red, brown, gray
HARDNESS	4
ENVIRONMENT	Hydrothermal cobalt-bearing deposits
OCCURRENCES	Africa, Australia, Canada, China, Germany, Morocco, Spain; Arizona, Utah, USA
VALUE	$20+ per specimen

Metaphysical Properties

Sphaerocobaltite is a mineral that promotes friendships and love, clearing the heart of past emotional traumas to make way for new possibilities in relationships. In psychic terms, Sphaerocobaltite may also assist in contact with spirit entities and opens up possibilities for spiritual vision and healings.

Sphalerite

ASTROLOGICAL SIGN

♊

Gemini

**VIBRATES TO
THE NUMBER(S)**

5 & 6

RULES

Root

Solar Plexus

Sexual/
Creative

Fluorite crystals on sphalerite from Cave-in-
Rock District, Illinois, USA, small cabinet.
Photo courtesy of Dr. Robert Lavinsky collection.

Sphalerite is zinc sulfide and forms as tetrahedral or pseudo-octahedral crystals, often with rounded edges, sometimes twinned; also as botryoidal, compact, granular, and cleavage masses. Sphalerite is transparent to translucent with an adamantine to submetallic luster, often fluorescent, and sometimes exhibiting the remarkable phenomenon of triboluminescence—emitting flashes of orange light when lightly stroked with a knife or stone. Sphalerite is the main ore of zinc and is usually found in association with galena, pyrite, and other sulfides along with calcite, dolomite, and fluorite. Sphalerite crystals of suitable size and transparency have been fashioned into gemstones, usually featuring the brilliant cut to best display sphalerite's high dispersion factor—over three times that of diamond. Owing to their softness and fragility the gems are often left unset and displayed instead as rare collector gems or museum pieces.

Sphalerite crystals on
matrix, Missouri, USA,
large cabinet.
Photo courtesy of Patti Polk collection.

Metaphysical Properties

Sphalerite is used for protection, decreasing stress, building confidence, and letting go of unwanted feelings or thoughts. It has been used to strengthen brain functions, treat disorders of the skin, and increase the libido. Sphalerite is also a cautious crystal in that it stimulates the user's ability to judge a possibly dangerous or deceitful situation and thus plan accordingly.

SYSTEM	Isometric
COLOR	Yellow, brown, red, green, black
HARDNESS	3.5-4
ENVIRONMENT	Sulfide ore veins, sedimentary deposits
OCCURRENCES	Australia, England, Czechoslovakia, Germany, Russia, Spain, Switzerland; Colorado, Illinois, Kansas, Missouri, Oklahoma, Tennessee, USA
VALUE	$30+ per specimen

Spinel

ASTROLOGICAL SIGN

↗ Sagittarius

♈ Aries

VIBRATES TO THE NUMBER

3

RULES

All Chakras

Spinel crystals on quartz from Burma, small cabinet.
Photo courtesy of Patti Polk, Travis Hartins collection.

Spinel is magnesium aluminum oxide and forms as small, perfect octahedrons, frequently twinned; also as aggregates of rounded grains. Spinel is transparent to opaque and has a vitreous luster. Throughout history spinel been cut as a gemstone and some spinels are among the world's most famous gemstones, such as the "Black Prince's Ruby" and the "Timur Ruby" in the British Crown Jewels, and the "Côte de Bretagne," formerly from the French Crown jewels. The Samarian Spinel is the largest known spinel in the world, weighing 500 carats. In the past, before the arrival of modern science, spinels and rubies were equally known as rubies until after the 18th century when the word ruby was only used for the red gem variety of the mineral corundum. Spinel crystals on matrix make distinctive and beautiful display specimens.

SYSTEM	Isometric
COLOR	Red, pink, blue, green, brown, black
HARDNESS	8
ENVIRONMENT	Plutonic and metamorphic rocks, alluvial and marine placer deposits
OCCURRENCES	Afghanistan, Africa, Burma, Italy, Madagascar, Sri Lanka; Montana, New Jersey, New York, USA
VALUE	$50+ per specimen

Metaphysical Properties

Spinel is a crystal that reveals the inherent beauty in all places—within the user, outside of the user, and within others. Spinel is a hopeful crystal that rejuvenates the user from within and provides gentle encouragement in all endeavors.

Spodumene

Spodumene is lithium aluminum silicate and forms as prismatic crystals, often flattened with longitudinal striations, columnar, and as rodlike aggregates of compact masses. Spodumene is translucent to transparent, has a vitreous to pearly luster, and is a trichroic mineral, changing color depending on the angle at which it is viewed. Spodumene occurs in lithium-rich granite pegmatites and aplites. Associated minerals include quartz, albite, petalite, eucryptite, lepidolite, and beryl. Spodumene is best known for its two most recognizable transparent gem crystal varieties, *hiddenite* and *kunzite*. Hiddenite is the green variety of spodumene, and kunzite is the lilac-pink variety. Both are usually cut and faceted as desirable gemstones. Spodumene is an important source of lithium and the non-gem variety tends toward an ashy, opaque, clouded appearance.

SYSTEM	Monoclinic
COLOR	Colorless, white, gray, yellow; Green (hiddenite), pink (kunzite)
HARDNESS	6.5-7
ENVIRONMENT	Pegmatites
OCCURRENCES	Afghanistan, Australia, Brazil, Canada, Mexico, Pakistan, Sweden; California, North Carolina, South Dakota, USA
VALUE	$20+ per specimen

Metaphysical Properties

Both varieties of spodumene offer an enhancement within the user to have loving thoughts that will direct the user's life in a most positive way. Hiddenite assists with intellectual and emotional pursuits, and Kunzite provides purification and a sense of peace.

Spodumene-Hiddenite

ASTROLOGICAL SIGN

♏
Scorpio

RULES

Heart

VIBRATES TO THE NUMBER

6

Spodumene var. hiddenite crystals on quartz with biotite from North Carolina, USA, cabinet. Photo courtesy of Patti Polk; Travis Hartins collection.

Spodumene-Kunzite

ASTROLOGICAL SIGN

♏
Scorpio

♉
Taurus

♌
Leo

**VIBRATES TO
THE NUMBER**

7

RULES

Heart

Spodumene var. kunzite crystal from
Tanzania, Africa, miniature.
Photo courtesy of Patti Polk; Kevin Burgart collection.

Staurolite

S

ASTROLOGICAL SIGN

♓

Pisces

VIBRATES TO
THE NUMBER

5

RULES

Heart

Third Eye

Crown

Staurolite crystal in matrix from New Mexico, USA, miniature.
Photo courtesy of Patti Polk; Dick Moore collection.

Staurolite is a basic silicate of iron and aluminum that forms as prismatic crystals with surfaces that are often rough or covered with an earthy coating caused by alteration, and frequently occur as two crystals intergrown or twinned at either 60- or 90-degree angles, forming a cruciform cross. Staurolite is translucent to opaque and has a vitreous to dull luster and occurs with almandine garnet, micas, kyanite, albite, biotite, and sillimanite in gneiss and schist of regional metamorphic rocks. Staurolite is also known by the name "Fairy Cross" and is generally considered a good luck charm.

SYSTEM	Orthorhombic
COLOR	Dark reddish-brown to blackish-brown, yellowish-brown, gray-brown
HARDNESS	7-7.5
ENVIRONMENT	Metamorphic rocks, pegmatites
OCCURRENCES	Brazil, Norway, Scotland, Switzerland; Georgia, Idaho, Minnesota, New Mexico, Virginia, USA
VALUE	$20+ per specimen

Metaphysical Properties

Staurolite is the four-leaf clover of crystals, enhancing good fortune and assisting in creating lucky opportunities. Staurolite can also provide relief from stress, depression, and addictive personality traits that harm the user's well-being.

206   The Crystal Guide

Stibnite

RULES

All
Chakras

Stibnite crystal cluster from Romania, miniature.
Photo courtesy of Patti Polk collection.

Stibnite is antimony sulfide and forms as prismatic or acicular crystals, elongated and striated parallel to the long axis; sometimes curved, bent, or twisted, also bladed, in radiating groups and columnar masses. Stibnite is opaque with a metallic luster, is sectile and slightly flexible, but not elastic. Stibnite will often have a tarnish of iridescent film on the surface. Small deposits of stibnite are common, but large deposits are rare. Pastes of antimony powder mixed with fat, known as kohl, have been used since ca. 3000 BC as cosmetics in the Middle East and surrounding regions. It was used to darken the brows and lashes, or to draw a line around the perimeter of the eye. Today, stibnite has many industrial uses, but it is most prized by collectors for its use as a mineral specimen due to its fine crystal structures.

SYSTEM	Orthorhombic
COLOR	Lead-gray, steel-gray
HARDNESS	2
ENVIRONMENT	Low temperature hydrothermal veins
OCCURRENCES	Canada, China, Germany, Italy, Japan, Mexico, Peru, Romania; Alaska, Arkansas, California, Idaho, Nevada, USA
VALUE	$15+ per specimen

Metaphysical Properties

Stibnite protects the user during meditative states from harmful and destructive entities that do not want the user to obtain enlightenment or higher thinking. Stibnite can also aid in attracting the relationships one desires, while removing those that are no longer necessary or draining.

Stilbite

ASTROLOGICAL SIGN

♈

Aries

VIBRATES TO THE NUMBER

33

Light pink stilbite crystals with green fluorapophyllite crystals from India, large cabinet.
Photo courtesy of Dr. Robert Lavinsky collection.

RULES

Heart

Third Eye

Crown

Stilbite is hydrated sodium calcium aluminum silicate and forms as prismatic crystals, usually in sheaflike, bow-tie, or bladed aggregates, often twinned; also as globular and fibrous radiating masses. Stilbite is transparent to translucent with a vitreous to pearly luster, and is a member of the zeolite group. Stilbite is a low-temperature secondary hydrothermal mineral and is often associated with other zeolites, prehnite, calcite, and quartz. Stibnite is sometimes used in the process of petroleum refining, but is mainly of interest to mineral collectors.

SYSTEM	Monoclinic
COLOR	Colorless, white, gray, pale yellow, pale pink, reddish-brown
HARDNESS	3.5-4
ENVIRONMENT	Cavities in basaltic or plutonic rocks, hydrothermal veins
OCCURRENCES	Brazil, Canada, Iceland, India, Scotland; New Jersey, North Carolina, USA
VALUE	$10+ per specimen

Metaphysical Properties

Stilbite provides the user with powerful, loving energy that can be used to strengthen relationships. Stilbite may also aid the user in ascending to the astral state so that, upon returning to this plane, the user can put to use the new knowledge learned during astral travel.

Sulfur

ASTROLOGICAL SIGN

♌

Leo

RULES

Solar Plexus

VIBRATES TO THE NUMBER

7

Single sulfur crystal from Italy, miniature. Photo courtesy of Patti Polk, Dick Moore collection.

Sulfur (also known as sulphur) is a native element and over 50 forms have been noted, blocky dipyramidal ones being most common, also tabular and spheroidal; also found as powdery coatings, encrustations, massive, and in reniform and stalactic forms. Sulfur is transparent to translucent and has an adamantine to greasy luster. Being abundant in native form, sulfur has been known since ancient times, being mentioned for its uses in ancient India, ancient Greece, Egypt, and in China where its earliest practical uses were in Chinese medicine, and later as an ingredient in gunpowder. Sulfur is referred to in the Bible as *brimstone*, probably due to its association with volcanic activity. In traditional skin treatments before the modern era of scientific medicine, elemental sulfur was used predominately in creams to alleviate conditions such as scabies, ringworm, psoriasis, eczema, and acne. Today, sulfur is mainly used to make sulfuric acid for a wide range of uses, particularly fertilizer. Sulfur is present in many types of meteorites and sulfur crystals make an attractive display specimen for mineral collectors due to their striking lemon-yellow color. Sulfur is also a powerful cleanser for the liver.

Sulfur crystals on celestite
from Poland, large cabinet.
Photo courtesy of Patti Polk,
Ray Pohlkotte collection.

Sulfur crystals with aragonite
from Italy, miniature. Photo courtesy
of Mike Keim collection.

SYSTEM	Orthorhombic
COLOR	Lemon-yellow, green or reddish yellow, orange, white
HARDNESS	1.5-2.5
ENVIRONMENT	Volcanic fumaroles, basalts, evaporative sedimentary deposits
OCCURRENCES	Bolivia, Canada, China, England, Italy, Japan, Poland, Sicily, Spain; Arkansas, California, Colorado, Nevada, Utah, USA
VALUE	$15+ per specimen

Metaphysical Properties

Sulfur offers calmness and resolution to those with anger issues that have plagued the user for many years. Sulfur promotes positive energy, inspiration, clearer mental processes, and the removal of distracting or negatively charged thoughts or emotions.

Titanite

ASTROLOGICAL SIGN

↗
Sagittarius

**VIBRATES TO
THE NUMBER**

4

RULES

Third Eye

Solar Plexus

Titanite crystal cluster from Minas Gerais, Brazil, small cabinet.
Photo courtesy of Dr. Robert Lavinsky collection.

Titanite (also known as *sphene*) is calcium titanium silicate and forms as prismatic, stubby, wedge-shaped and flattened crystals, sometimes twinned, or tabular and platy. Titanite is transparent to translucent, has an adamantine to resinous luster, and is an ore of titanium. Transparent titanite crystals are noted for their strong trichroism, the three colors presented being dependent on body color. As a gemstone, titanite is usually some shade of yellow-green, but can be brown or black. Hue depends on iron content, with low iron content causing green and yellow colors, and high iron content causing brown or black hues. Color zoning is typical in titanite, and it is prized for its exceptional dispersive power, which exceeds that of diamond. Jewelry use of titanite is limited, both because the stone is uncommon in gem quality and is relatively soft. Titanite is a source of titanium dioxide, a mineral often used in the manufacture of paint pigments.

Titanite twinned crystals on matrix from Minas Gerais, Brazil, small cabinet. Photo courtesy of Dr. Robert Lavinsky collection.

Metaphysical Properties

Titanite acts as a calming agent that refreshes and clears the mind in productive ways. Titanite is useful for people, such as students, who are taking in a great deal of new information as it assists with memory and the assimilation of the new information into one's knowledge base. Titanite also strengthens the will and aids in the manifestation of one's desires.

SYSTEM	Monoclinic
COLOR	Reddish-brown, green, yellow, gray, brown, black
HARDNESS	5-5.5
ENVIRONMENT	Felsic igneous rocks, metamorphic rocks, pegmatites
OCCURRENCES	Brazil, Canada, China, Italy, Pakistan, Russia, Switzerland; California, Montana, New Jersey, New York, USA
VALUE	$30+ per specimen

Topaz

ASTROLOGICAL SIGN

↗
Sagittarius

RULES

Solar Plexus

Third Eye

**VIBRATES TO
THE NUMBER**

6

Sherry-colored topaz crystals with
hematite inclusions from Topaz
Mountain, Utah, USA, miniature.
Photo courtesy of Dr. Robert Lavinsky collection.

Topaz is aluminum fluorosilicate and usually forms as stubby to medium-long prismatic crystals striated lengthwise, often terminated by pyramidal faces. Pure topaz is transparent to translucent, has a vitreous luster, and is generally colorless except when tinted by impurities. Throughout history topaz has been used primarily as a gemstone, with no other viable commercial applications. Typical *Golden topaz* ranges in color from golden yellow to golden brown, and Brazilian *Imperial topaz* can often have a bright yellow to deep golden brown hue, sometimes even violet. Many brown or pale topazes are treated to make them bright yellow, gold, pink, or violet colored. Some Imperial topaz stones can fade on exposure to sunlight after an extended period of time. Naturally occurring blue topaz is quite rare, and often colorless, gray, pale yellow, or light blue material is heat treated and irradiated to produce a more desired darker blue. A variety of topaz called "Mystic Topaz" is colorless topaz which has been artificially coated with mineral salts giving it the iridescent rainbow effect, and sometimes, citrine quartz is passed off as faceted topaz, so be cautious when purchasing topaz gemstones.

Imperial Topaz

Metaphysical Properties: If used with the intention to store energy, ideas, and feelings of love, this stone acts as a rechargeable battery that can provide the user with a boost of stamina and mental liveliness. Imperial topaz is also a crystal of faith that may assist the user in reaching an enlightened state by keeping their focus not just in the physical plane, but also on higher levels.

Blue Topaz

Metaphysical Properties: Blue topaz is a rather objective, clear-thinking crystal that reminds the user to not be arrogant, selfish, or blinded by passion when contemplating the inner self as well as when communicating with others.

SYSTEM	Orthorhombic
COLOR	Colorless, yellow, blue, green, violet, brown, orange, pink
HARDNESS	8
ENVIRONMENT	Igneous rocks, granite pegmatites, placers
OCCURRENCES	Africa, Brazil, China, Mexico, Pakistan, Russia, Sri Lanka; California, Colorado, New Hampshire, Utah, USA
VALUE	$40+ per specimen

Metaphysical Properties
White or colorless topaz helps the user to achieve clarity in their intentions and to align those intentions to Divine Will. Topaz enables the user with the ability to express their spiritual energy through their creations and to manifest one's vision to fruition.

Imperial Topaz

ASTROLOGICAL SIGN

Sagittarius

Leo

Pisces

RULES

Solar Plexus

VIBRATES TO THE NUMBER

9

Single Imperial topaz crystal from Brazil, miniature.
Photo courtesy of Mike Keim.

Blue Topaz

ASTROLOGICAL SIGN

Sagittarius

Virgo

RULES

Throat

Third Eye

VIBRATES TO THE NUMBER

3

Rare blue topaz crystal from St. Annes Mine, Zimbabwe, miniature.
Photo courtesy of Dr. Robert Lavinsky collection.

Tourmaline Group

ASTROLOGICAL SIGN

♎︎

Libra

VIBRATES TO THE NUMBER

2

RULES

All Chakras

Bi-color elbaite tourmaline crystal from the Himalaya Mine, San Diego, California, USA, miniature.
Photo courtesy of Patti Polk collection.

The tourmaline group is a series of complex silicates of boron and aluminum whose composition varies widely due to a number of different mineral substitutions. Tourmaline occurs as long, slender to thick prismatic and columnar crystals that are usually triangular in cross-section, often with curved striated faces. The style of termination at the ends of crystals is sometimes asymmetrical, called hemimorphism. Small slender prismatic crystals are common in a fine-grained granite called aplite, often forming radial daisy-like patterns. Tourmaline is distinguished by its three-sided prisms; no other common mineral has three sides. Prisms faces often have heavy vertical striations that produce a rounded triangular effect. Tourmaline is transparent to translucent, and has a vitreous to resinous luster. Some varieties of tourmaline exhibit the characteristics of *pleochroism* (color-changing) or *chatoyance* (a moving band of reflected light when cut into a cabochon). Tourmaline is also both pyroelectric and piezoelectric. If a specimen is put under a pressure or temperature change, it will generate an electrical charge. When this happens, dust particles become attached to the crystal ends.

The tourmaline varieties are:

Elbaite: Sodium lithium aluminum rich. Colors: Pink to red (var. rubellite), green-pink bicolor (known as watermelon), blue (var. indicolite), green.

Schorl: Sodium iron rich. Colors: Dark greenish-black, black (usually opaque).

Buergerite: Sodium iron rich. Colors: Brown, black.

Dravite: Sodium magnesium rich. Colors: Brown.

Uvite: Calcium magnesium iron aluminum rich. Colors: Green, greenish-black, black, brown.

Liddicoatite: Calcium lithium aluminum rich. Colors: Green, pink.

Tourmaline has been appreciated as a gemstone since earliest times and is an extremely popular specimen mineral among collectors today. It is one of the most multicolored mineral types known, occurring in almost every color of the spectrum. Individual stones are often multicolored and are unsurpassed in their beauty. The color of some tourmaline can be enhanced through heat treatment. Some greenish stones can be made deep green, some brownish-red stones can be made red, and some light pink stones can be made colorless through heating, so be aware of any heat treatment processes if you are planning on buying gemstones for jewelry making.

Rubellite Tourmaline

Metaphysical Properties: Rubellite promotes a willingness within the user to respond with love and tact to others. This crystal also stimulates a love-centered consciousness that affects the whole body.

Watermelon Tourmaline

Metaphysical Properties: This type of tourmaline allows the user to find the humor and benefits of unpleasant experiences in order to be able to transmute the negative experience into a positive one. Watermelon tourmaline supports cooperation as opposed to combativeness.

Indicolite Tourmaline

Metaphysical Properties: Indicolite urges the user to seek the opportunity to help others through teaching and loving. Harmony is the ultimate aim with this crystal; it wants the user to find peace on this plane.

Metaphysical Properties

Each specific color or type of this crystal offers different effects, but as a whole it can provide the user with self-confidence and the ability to reverse the idea of being a victim in life to a survivor, in spite of past negative experiences. Tourmaline is also a balancer of the body and mind, which yields a resilience within the user to negativity or unhealthiness, and promotes positive thinking.

SYSTEM	Trigonal
COLOR	Red, pink, green, blue, brown, black, bi-colored
HARDNESS	7-7.5
ENVIRONMENT	Granite pegmatites, metamorphic rocks, hypothermal veins
OCCURRENCES	Africa, Australia, Brazil, Canada, Italy, Madagascar, Russia, Sri Lanka; California, Maine, New Jersey, New York, North Carolina, USA
VALUE	$40+ per specimen

Schorl Tourmaline

Metaphysical Properties: Schorl is both a repellent and powerful protector against negative energies and thoughts. Schorl also provides resilience against depressive or damaging emotions.

Dravite Tourmaline

Metaphysical Properties: Grounds the user in the physical plane both during times of stress and post-meditation. Dravite also acts as a cleanser and stamina-provider after a strenuous day.

Uvite Tourmaline

Metaphysical Properties: Uvite provides balance between dualities (the body and the earth, the left and right side of the brain, etc.). Aside from balancing, uvite also grounds the user through understanding responsibility, the importance of consequences, and the difference between action and non-action.

Rubellite Tourmaline

ASTROLOGICAL SIGN

Sagittarius

Scorpio

VIBRATES TO
THE NUMBER(S)
**1, 2,
4 & 5**

RULES

Root

Heart

Elbaite var. rubellite crystal on feldspar from
the Himalaya Mine, San Diego, California,
USA, cabinet specimen.
Photo courtesy of Dr. Robert Lavinsky collection.

Watermelon Tourmaline

ASTROLOGICAL SIGN

Virgo

Gemini

**VIBRATES TO
THE NUMBER**

2

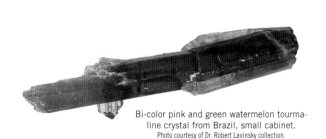

Bi-color pink and green watermelon tourmaline crystal from Brazil, small cabinet.
Photo courtesy of Dr. Robert Lavinsky collection.

RULES

Heart

Indicolite Tourmaline

ASTROLOGICAL SIGN

Libra

Taurus

**VIBRATES TO
THE NUMBER**

6

Indicolite crystal intergrown
within citrine quartz from
Brazil, small cabinet. Photo
courtesy of Kevin Burgart collection.

RULES

Throat

Third Eye

Schorl Tourmaline

ASTROLOGICAL SIGN

Capricorn

**VIBRATES TO
THE NUMBER(S)**

3 & 4

Black tourmaline var. schorl
crystals in mica from the
Tripp Mine, New Hampshire,
USA, small cabinet. Photo courtesy
of Larry Michon collection.

RULES

Root

T

Dravite Tourmaline

ASTROLOGICAL SIGN

Aries

**VIBRATES TO
THE NUMBER(S)**

2 & 9

RULES

Root

Heart

Dravite crystals with mica from Brazil, miniature.
Photo courtesy of Kevin Burgart collection.

Uvite Tourmaline

ASTROLOGICAL SIGN

Sagittarius

**VIBRATES TO
THE NUMBER**

5

RULES

Root

Uvite crystals with a magnesite rhomb from Brazil, miniature.
Photo courtesy of Dr. Robert Lavinsky collection.

Ulexite

ASTROLOGICAL SIGN

♊

Gemini

RULES

Third Eye

**VIBRATES TO
THE NUMBER**

8

Ulexite crystal from California, small cabinet.
Photo courtesy of Patti Polk collection.

Ulexite is hydrous sodium calcium borate and usually occurs as rounded, lens-like crystalline masses of hair-like parallel fibers, and as "cotton ball" tufts of acicular crystals. Ulexite is transparent to translucent, has a silky luster, and may be chatoyant. Ulexite is also known as "TV Rock" due to its unusual optical characteristics. The fibers of ulexite act as optical fibers, transmitting light along their lengths by internal reflection. When a piece of ulexite is cut with flat polished faces perpendicular to the orientation of the fibers, a good-quality specimen will display an image of whatever surface is adjacent to its other side. Ulexite is an ore of boron and is used in the manufacture of glass wool.

SYSTEM	Triclinic
COLOR	Colorless, white
HARDNESS	2.5
ENVIRONMENT	Evaporite environments
OCCURRENCES	Argentina, Chile, Peru; California, USA
VALUE	$5+ per specimen

Metaphysical Properties

Ulexite is a mineral ideal for those who struggle to find solutions to both broad and narrow problems within the user's daily life. Ulexite also acts as a stimulator for a person's innate psychic abilities to be awakened and utilized while on the physical plane.

Vanadinite

ASTROLOGICAL SIGN

♍

Virgo

VIBRATES TO THE NUMBER

9

Vanadinite crystals on matrix from Morocco, large cabinet.
Photo courtesy of Dr. Robert Lavinsky collection.

RULES

Root

Solar Plexus

Third Eye

Sexual/
Creative

Vanadinite is lead chlorovanadate and forms as small, hexagonal prisms, usually barrel-shaped, sometimes hollow; also as acicular, fibrous, hairlike radiated masses or crusts. Vanadinite is transparent to translucent, has an adamantine to resinous luster, and is frequently found in association with galena, wulfenite, limonite, and barite. Vanadinite is a secondary mineral found in arid climates and forms by oxidation of primary lead minerals. Vanadinite is an ore of vanadium and is a member of the apatite group. Vanadinite mineral specimens can be quite beautiful and are a welcome addition to any collector's display.

SYSTEM	Hexagonal
COLOR	Bright red, orange-red, red-brown, brown, yellow
HARDNESS	3
ENVIRONMENT	Oxidation zone of lead deposits
OCCURRENCES	Africa, Argentina, Austria, Mexico, Morocco; Arizona, California, Montana, New Mexico, USA
VALUE	$15+ per specimen

Metaphysical Properties

Vanadinite assists in bringing order to a disordered life through a change in the user's mentality, and can help with defining short and long-term goals to better fit the user's creative energies. Vanadinite may also help an obsessive over-spender learn frugality, especially if any issues in the user's life involve monetary concerns.

Vanadinite crystals on barite matrix
from the North Geronimo Mine,
Arizona, USA, cabinet specimen.
Photo courtesy of Patti Polk collection.

Vivianite

RULES

Heart

Solar Plexus

Vivianite crystal from Bolivia, miniature.
Photo courtesy of Patti Polk; Dick Moore collection.

Vivianite is hydrous iron phosphate and forms as flattened, elongated prismatic crystals, that may be rounded or corroded; and as stellate groups or encrustations with a bladed or fibrous structure. Vivianite is transparent to translucent with a vitreous to pearly luster. Vivianite is a secondary mineral found in a number of geologic environments such as the oxidation zone of metal ore deposits, in granite pegmatites containing phosphate minerals, in clays and sediments, and in recent alluvial deposits replacing organic material such as peat, lignite, bog iron ores, and forest soils. Fossil bones and teeth buried in peat bogs are sometimes replaced by vivianite. Vivianite may darken to a deep blue color when exposed to light over time. Vivianite crystals make striking display pieces and are prized by collectors.

SYSTEM	Monoclinic
COLOR	Colorless, green, blue
HARDNESS	1.5-2
ENVIRONMENT	Oxidation zone of sulfide deposits
OCCURRENCES	Bolivia, Brazil, Canada, England, Germany; Colorado, Idaho, Maine, Utah, Virginia, USA
VALUE	$30+ per specimen

Metaphysical Properties

Vivianite helps to attune one to the deeper urgings of their heart's desire and to aid oneself in entering a state of enlightened compassion. Vivianite helps to dispel disharmonious energies from the auric field and to remove negativity from one's thought patterns.

Wavellite

ASTROLOGICAL SIGN

♒♒
Aquarius

**VIBRATES TO
THE NUMBER**

1

RULES

Brow Chakra

Wavellite radial aggregate crystals in matrix
from High Down Quarry, England, small cabinet.
Photo courtesy of Dr. Robert Lavinsky collection.

Wavellite is hydrous aluminum phosphate and generally forms as spherulitic, radiating aggregates made up of small, fibrous crystals, and as botryoidal crusts; and rarely as stout, prismatic, striated crystals. Wavellite is transparent to translucent, has a vitreous to silky luster and often occurs in fissures of rocks rich in aluminum, and may be associated with variscite, turquoise, limonite, and quartz. When wavellite is available in economically productive amounts it is used in the making of phosphate fertilizers, otherwise is it generally appreciated as a mineral specimen.

SYSTEM	Orthorhombic
COLOR	Light green, yellow-green, white, gray, brown
HARDNESS	3.5-4
ENVIRONMENT	Zone of alteration of metamorphic rocks, pegmatites
OCCURRENCES	Bolivia, Brazil, England; Arkansas, Colorado, Pennsylvania, USA
VALUE	$10+ per specimen

Metaphysical Properties

Wavellite helps a person to look at the overall "big picture" before making any important decisions. Wavellite also assists one in managing difficult situations and provides information relevant to choosing an appropriate solution depending on the best method for accomplishing the task.

Radiating wavellite
crystals in matrix from
Arkansas, small cabinet.
Photo courtesy of Patti Polk collection.

Wulfenite

ASTROLOGICAL SIGN

♐

Sagittarius

RULES

Solar Plexus

Sexual/
Creative

**VIBRATES TO
THE NUMBER**

7

Wulfenite crystal specimen
from the Red Cloud Mine,
Arizona, USA, thumbnail.
Photo courtesy of Patti Polk collection.

Wulfenite is lead molybdate and forms as stubby, pyramidal crystals, often thin and tabular with a square outline; sometimes pseudo-tetragonal due to twinning, and as granular aggregates. Wulfenite is transparent to translucent, heavy, and has an adamantine to resinous luster. It occurs as a secondary mineral in oxidized hydrothermal lead deposits. It occurs with cerussite, anglesite, smithsonite, hemimorphite, vanadinite, pyromorphite, mimetite, descloizite, and various iron and manganese oxides. Wulfenite was first described in 1845 for an occurrence in Bad Bleiberg, Carinthia, Austria, and was named for Franz Xavier von Wulfen (1728–1805), an Austrian mineralogist. In the United States, a well-respected locality for excellent, well-formed, wulfenite crystals is the Red Cloud Mine in Arizona, with specimens exhibiting a deep red-orange color. Specimens from this location are highly prized by collectors and are found in museums and fine mineral collections worldwide.

Wulfenite crystal cluster from
Arizona, USA, miniature.
Photo courtesy of Patti Polk collection.

Metaphysical Properties

Wulfenite acts as a mediator between the user and the spiritual world to provide for fluid connectivity between the two. Wulfenite also promotes a healthy acceptance of the existence of negative energies, allowing the individual, through this awareness, to circumvent any limitations to advancement by not allowing the issue to impede their progress.

SYSTEM	Tetragonal
COLOR	Red-orange, yellow-orange, honey yellow, yellow-brown
HARDNESS	3
ENVIRONMENT	Oxidation zone of lead deposits
OCCURRENCES	Austria, Mexico, Morocco, Romania; Arizona, Colorado, New Mexico, Pennsylvania, USA
VALUE	$40+ per specimen

Zincite

ASTROLOGICAL SIGN

Libra

Taurus

**VIBRATES TO
THE NUMBER**

5

RULES

Root

Solar Plexus

Sexual/
Creative

Zincite crystals in calcite matrix from the Franklin
Mine, New Jersey, USA, small cabinet.
Photo courtesy of Dr. Robert Lavinsky collection.

Zincite is zinc oxide and commonly forms as granular compact or disseminated masses, and rarely as small pyramidal crystals, often rounded and corroded. Zincite is transparent to semi-opaque with an adamantine to dull luster. The most well-known location for zincite in the U.S. is at the Franklin mining district in New Jersey, where it occurs with fluorescent calcite, wilemite, and franklinite. Beautiful zincite crystals can be grown artificially as a by-product of zinc smelting, such as are found at the zinc smelters in Poland. Synthetic crystals can be colorless or can range in color from dark red, orange, or yellow to olive green. Both natural and synthetic zincite crystals are significant for their early use as semiconductor crystal detectors in the early development of crystal radios before the advent of vacuum tubes. The zincite specimens from the Franklin mines in New Jersey, USA, are collected as attractive mineral specimens in their own right, and the crystals from Poland are highly sought after by collectors for their beauty and use as a metaphysical stone.

Zincite crystal
from Poland,
miniature.
Photo courtesy of
Patti Polk collection.

Metaphysical Properties

Zincite acts as a type of magnet to attract the user to other individuals with similar opinions and thought processes. On the physical plane, zincite is also helpful for bringing together lovers on the physical plane, and can assist already existing relationships on a sexual level.

SYSTEM	Hexagonal
COLOR	Dark red, orange, yellow, green, white
HARDNESS	4
ENVIRONMENT	Metamorphic rocks, pegmatites, intrusive magmatic rocks
OCCURRENCES	Africa, Australia, China, Germany, Italy, Poland; Arizona, California, New Jersey, Nevada, Utah, USA
VALUE	$40+ per specimen

Zircon

ASTROLOGICAL SIGN

Virgo

Leo

Sagittarius

**VIBRATES TO
THE NUMBER**

4

Tetragonal zircon crystal from
South Carolina, USA, thumbnail.
Photo courtesy of Dr. Robert Lavinsky collection.

RULES

All
Chakras

Zircon is zirconium silicate and forms as stubby, prismatic, sometimes dipyramidal crystals, or more commonly as disseminated grains. Zircon is transparent to opaque with an adamantine to greasy luster. Zircon is a major rock forming constituent in the crust of the Earth and occurs as a common accessory mineral in igneous rocks (as primary crystallization products), in metamorphic rocks, and as detrital grains in sedimentary rocks. Their average size in granite rocks is about 0.1-0.3 mm, but they can also grow to sizes of several centimeters, especially in mafic pegmatites and carbonatites. Large zircon crystals are rare, and when they are of sufficient color and clarity, are cut and faceted as gemstones for use in jewelry making.

SYSTEM	Tetragonal
COLOR	Colorless, yellow, reddish-brown, brown, blue, green, gray
HARDNESS	7.5
ENVIRONMENT	Metamorphic rocks, pegmatites, igneous rocks, sedimentary deposits
OCCURRENCES	Canada, France, Germany, Norway, Russia, Sri Lanka, Sweden; Arkansas, California, Connecticut, Idaho, Maine, Massachusetts, North & South Carolina, USA
VALUE	$40+ per specimen

Metaphysical Properties

Zircon promotes the union of physical, mental, emotional, and spiritual elements within the user to create an internal harmony that allows for innovation and clear-thinking. Zircon also acts to increase one's resolve and willingness to accomplish their chosen goals in life's endeavors.

Zoisite

ASTROLOGICAL SIGN

♊

Gemini

VIBRATES TO THE NUMBER

4

RULES

Root

Heart

Third Eye

Zoisite is hydrous calcium aluminum silicate and forms as elongated, prismatic crystals, finely striated on the prism faces, often poorly terminated; also as bladed or columnar aggregates and as granular masses. Zoisite is transparent to semi-opaque with a vitreous to pearly luster on cleavage surfaces. Zoisite occurs in a number of colors depending on the included minerals and each are distinguished according to their various colors and physical forms. Blue-violet, transparent, gem-quality zoisite is known as the gemstone *tanzanite*, and is highly prized when cut and faceted for jewelry making. Massive green zoisite, often included with ruby crystals, is known as *anyolite*, and is popular for carving, as is *thulite*, a massive pink variety is also suitable for carving. All types of zoisite are collectible as mineral specimens and many are valued as metaphysical stones.

Tanzanite

Additional properties: Tanzanite stimulates the Throat, Third Eye, and Crown chakras, bringing together both the ability to communicate and personal psychic power that enables the user to voice their visions appropriately.

Anyolite

Additional properties: Anyolite stimulates the Root and Heart chakras, giving one the courage and energy for growth and rebirth on all levels. Anyolite supports the reproductive process both physically and spiritually.

Thulite

Additional properties: Thulite encourages the emotion of joy, enthusiasm, and excitement of life. Thulite is a good stone to carry with you if you are seeking to make new friends or find a romantic partner. Thulite rules the Heart, Sexual/Creative, Solar Plexus, and Throat chakras.

Zoisite var. tanzanite crystal from Tanzania, Africa, thumbnail. Photo courtesy of Patti Polk; William Horton collection.

Massive green zoisite var. anyolite with included ruby crystals
from India, cabinet size.
Photo courtesy of Patti Polk collection.

Pink zoisite var. thulite crystals with
quartz from Norway, miniature.
Photo courtesy of John Sobolewski collection.

SYSTEM	Orthorhombic
COLOR	Colorless, pink, green, blue-violet, greenish gray, yellowish brown
HARDNESS	6-6.5
ENVIRONMENT	Metamorphic rocks, hydrothermal veins
OCCURRENCES	Africa, Austria, Australia, Canada, China, Norway; California, Colorado, Montana, Nevada, New Mexico, North Carolina, Virginia, USA
VALUE	$20+ per specimen

Metaphysical Properties

Zoisite creates positive force fields around the user to ward off negative energies from outside forces. Internally, this crystal helps reduce negativity and harmful thoughts that limit the user's ability to utilize their talents and innate abilities.

Glossary

Acicular: An aggregate of long, slender, crystals (i.e. natrolite). This term is also used to describe the crystal habit of single long, thin, slender crystals.

Adamantine (luster): Transparent minerals with a very high luster are said to have an adamantine luster. (Translucent to nearly opaque minerals with a very high luster are said to have a submetallic luster.)

Adularescence: An effect seen on certain minerals that causes it to display a billowy, rounded, ghost-like reflection with a bluish-whitish color emanating from the surface when the mineral is cut into a cabochon. It is caused by structural anomalies or build-up of water in the mineral. The minerals most famous for exhibiting adularescence are opal and moonstone, and the name is derived from adularia, of which moonstone is a variety.

Aggregate: A grouping of crystals. Aggregates are defined by the ways crystals are clustered together.

Amorphous: Without a definitive crystalline shape.

Association: When more than one mineral is found in combination with another mineral in one specimen they are said to be "in association."

Aqueous: Formed from precipitating hard water. Stalagmites and stalactites are common examples.

Asterism: Effect exhibited on some minerals (usually only visible in polished cabochons) causing it to reflect a billowy, star-like formation of concentrated light that moves around when the mineral is rotated. Asterism is caused by dense inclusions of tiny, parallel, slender, fibers in the mineral that cause the light to reflect in such an interesting manner. Minerals that display asterism may exhibit four, six, and sometimes twelve-rayed "stars," depending on the inclusions, size, and facet mode. Some specimens may display much stronger asterism than others, and some specimens may have areas where the inclusions are not present, leaving holes or empty areas in the star.

Aventurescence: The effect caused by small inclusions of a mineral with a highly reflective surface (commonly hematite, pyrite, or goethite) that create a glistening effect, as if it is pasted with glitter, when rotated or looked at from different positions. The name is derived from aventurine, a green micaceous variety of quartz that exhibits this effect.

Axis: Imaginary line drawn through the center of an object, either horizontally or vertically. In the case of minerals, it is used to determine if and how mineral has symmetry. The horizontal axis is known as the x axis; the vertical axis, as the y axis. Axis lines are usually drawn as dotted lines.

Banding: The presence of color zoning lines, or "bands," in some minerals.

Birefringence: The optical property of a material having a refractive index that depends on the polarization and propagation direction of light. Double refraction.

Bladed: Crystal habit describing flat, elongated, "knife-like" crystals (i.e. kyanite).

Botryoidal: Aggregate resembling a cluster of grapes. Also known as globular. Rounded ball-like aggregates that are smaller in size than reniform and mammilary agglomerations.

Boule: Synthetic gems created from molten liquids placed in tear shaped molds to crystallize, leaving them with a tear-like form. Mostly applied to synthetic rubies and sapphires.

Cabochon: Gemstone without facets that is highly polished, domed, and has smooth, rounded edges.

Carat: Weight measurement used in reference to gemstones in regard to their evaluation. A carat is .2 grams (or 200 milligrams), and this weight is used worldwide, even in the U.S., where the metric system isn't used. A point is the weight used only in reference to very small, precious gemstones, and represents 1/100th of a carat. The abbreviation for carat is Ct. and for point is Pt. The term carat in regard to gemstones should not be confused with the term carat in regard to gold. When referring to gold, it means the content of gold a gold ornament contains. Because of the confusion, the term carat in regard to gold has been changed to karat.

Cat's eye: A mineral with dense inclusions of tiny, parallel, slender, fibers that may cause it to exhibit chatoyancy. The most notable cat's eye mineral is chrysoberyl cat's eye, which is known simply as cat's eye.

Chatoyancy: A phenomenon of certain cat's eye minerals that cause it to exhibit a concentrated narrow band of reflected light across the center of the mineral. Chatoyancy is usually only seen on polished cabochons.

Cleavage: The splitting or tendency of a crystal to split along definite crystalline planes to produce smooth surfaces.

Cluster: Dense agglomeration of crystals.

Columnar: Aggregate defining a mineral that has parallel, slender, compact, adjoining crystals.

Coralloidal: Coral-like branching and twisting forms.

Crazing: Condition in opal that causes it to form small, internal cracks, and in some severe cases will eventually disintegrate the opal.

Crystal system: The primary method of classification of crystals. The crystal system classifies crystals in six groups: isometric, tetragonal, hexagonal (which includes trigonal), orthorhombic, monoclinic, and triclinic.

Crystalline: Having a crystal structure.

Dendritic: Having a tree-like appearance or habit.

Dichroism: Literally means "two colors." A mineral that exhibits one color when viewed from one angle but a different color when viewed from a different angle is said to display dichroism.

Double refraction: Phenomenon exhibited on all non-opaque minerals except for amorphous ones and ones that crystallize in the isometric system. A light ray enters the crystal and splits into two rays, making anything observed through the crystal appear as double. The double refraction on most minerals is so weak that it cannot be observed without special instruments. However, in some minerals, such as the Iceland spar variety of calcite, it is strongly seen. The double refraction is different in every mineral and, thus, can be used to identify gems. Double refraction is measured with a refractometer.

Doubly terminated: Exhibiting a pointed crystal figure on both terminations.

Druse or Druzy: A fine coating of tiny crystals covering the surface of a host rock.

Ductile: The ability of a metal to be drawn into a wire.

Dull (luster): The luster of minerals with little reflectiveness.

Earthy (luster): Luster describing minerals that are microcrystalline or amorphous and have non-reflective surfaces.

Elongated: Describing a crystal with a lengthened side, meaning that one side is far longer in one direction.

Environment: Area or region conducive for the development of a mineral. Certain minerals only develop in certain environments.

Etched: Crystal faces which have been modified by scarring or pitting caused by a secondary chemical action.

Euhedral: A crystal that exhibits good, well-formed faces.

Evaporate: A mineral formed by the evaporation of saline water.

Even (fracture): Mineral fracture forming a smooth, flat surface.

Face: A flat plane on the surface of a crystalline form.

Facet: A singular flat surface displayed in a gem. It may grow naturally but is usually hand cut. This definition includes the meaning of a specific cut for gems.

Feldspar: Group of minerals that are aluminum silicates containing potassium, sodium, and/or calcium.

Fibrous: Aggregate describing a mineral constructed of fine, usually parallel threads. Some fibrous minerals contain cloth-like flexibility, meaning they can be bent and feel like cotton.

Floater: A crystal with no visible point of attachment or connection to a matrix.

Fluorescence: A natural phenomenon of neon luminescence created within a mineral when lit by ultraviolet light.

Foliated: Made up of thin, separable leaves or laminae, like a book.

Form: The physical appearance of all the crystal faces and structure of a mineral.

Fracture: The characteristic way a mineral breaks when placed under stress, aside from cleavage.

Geode: Hollow rock filled or partially filled with crystals.

Globular: The term globular is used as a synonym of botryoidal, but sometimes describes any rounded agglomeration, such as botryoidal, reniform, and mammilary.

Granular: Containing grains, or in grains, as sand.

Group: The classification order of minerals based on their chemical structure.

Gwindel: A twisted, corkscrew, or spiral pattern of growth habit seen in certain crystals.

Habit: The attributes of the appearance of a crystal or aggregate.

Hackly (fracture): Type of fracture resembling broken metal, exhibiting sharp, jagged surfaces. This fracture is sometimes also known as a "jagged" fracture.

Hopper: A crystal form that has stepped, indented, or hollowed cavities on its faces.

Hydrothermal: Minerals formed by the action of water and heat.

Igneous rock: A type of rock from volcanic origins. Igneous rock can be glassy, crystalline, or both.

Inclusion: A crystal, mineral, or fragment of another substance enclosed within a crystal or rock.

Iridescence: Light effect causing a mineral to display a play of colors on an apparently plain surface. Iridescence is also the result of mild tarnishing of a few metallic lustered minerals, such as chalcopyrite and hematite.

Japanese Law twin: Form of contact twinning in which two single quartz crystals are joined by their base at an angle near 90 degrees.

Labradorescence: Effect that causes dark, metallic-like color shimmers, commonly blue and green, to be displayed on a few minerals. The name is derived from labradorite, a mineral that produces the best example of this effect.

Lenticular: Lens shaped. When applied to minerals, it refers to concretions or nodules that have a flattened, lens-like shape.

Luster: The way in which a mineral shines due to reflected light.

Macrocrystalline: Crystals that are large enough to be seen by the naked eye.

Malleable: A metal that can be flattened or stretched out by pounding and not break.

Mammilary: Aggregate describing smooth, rounded, agglomerations.

Massive: Term used to describe a rock or mineral that has no definitive shape and lacks any outward appearance of crystal structure or form.

Matrix: A bed or base of host rock where additional minerals have formed or crystals are attached onto its surface.

Metal: Any of a category of electropositive elements or combinations of them in the form of minerals that exhibit a metallic luster, malleability, ductility, and conductivity.

Metallic (luster): Exhibiting the luster of a metal, which is opaque and highly reflective.

Metamorphic: Mineral environment in which the minerals are secondary in origin, forming from alteration through heat and pressure.

Microcrystalline: Composed of tiny crystals that can only be seen with a microscope.

Native Elements: Group of approximately 30 minerals naturally occurring with a molecular structure of only one element, such as copper, gold, and silver.

Non-crystalline: Not containing any crystals; amorphous, massive.

Occurrence: The area where a particular mineral is found.

Oolitic: Aggregate composed of very small, spherical particles.

Optical properties: Physical properties of a mineral or gem that have to do with optics, such as dispersion, absorption spectra, refractive index, asterism, and dichroism, to name a few.

Ore: Material that has a valuable constituent, usually a precious metal, that makes it profitable for extraction.

Oxidation: The process of undergoing a chemical change through exposure to oxygen.

Paramorph: A pseudomorph involving two minerals with an identical composition but different crystal structures. The original mineral forms, but conditions then cause it to become unstable, so it transforms into the other mineral with the same chemical structure while retaining the original crystal shape.

Pearly (luster): Exhibiting a shimmering luster similar to the inside of a mollusk shell or pearl.

Pegmatite: An intrusive igneous body of variable grain size that often includes coarse or large crystal growths.

Phenocryst: A relatively large crystal embedded in the groundmass of another rock.

Phosphorescence: The ability of some fluorescent minerals to continue glowing for several seconds after an ultraviolet source has been removed.

Piezoelectric: A crystal that becomes electrically charged by pressure.

Pisolitic: Aggregate composed of small, spherical balls, larger in size than in oolitic specimens.

Pleochroism: The effect present in a mineral exhibiting two or more separate colors when viewed at different angles. Pleochroism and dichroism are similar, but dichroism refers only to two colors, but pleochroism can be more than two.

Platy: A mineral habit with overlapping thin, flat scales or crystals.

Porphry: Igneous rock containing large, noticeable crystals, usually feldspars.

Prismatic: Crystal habit describing a crystal with four or more sides similar in length and width. Prismatic crystals are usually elongated in one direction.

Pseudomorph: A mineral or organic substance that is replaced by another mineral yet retains its original shape.

Pyroelectric: A mineral or crystal that becomes electrically charged by temperature changes.

Radiating: Aggregate composed of tiny, slender crystals compacted together radiating from a central point. The radiation can be flat or three-dimensional. If three-dimensional, this aggregate commonly occurs with circular, ball-like masses, and is known as spherulitic.

Refraction: The splitting of white light into the colors of the spectrum.

Reniform: Aggregate describing smooth, rounded, kidney-like agglomerations.

Resinous (luster): Having a greasy or resin-like sheen.

Reticulated: Aggregate composed of long crystals in a net-like form in which all the crystals crisscross each other.

Reverse scepter crystal: A prismatic crystal that shows thick growth at its center or base with a slender end termination.

Rough: Rocks as found in the field. In regard to gemstones, it refers to unfaceted material.

Scepter crystal: A crystal that exhibits a symmetrical cap of one crystal that has grown over and enveloped the end termination of a thinner, base crystal.

Schiller: The *schiller effect* is a shimmering play of colors resulting from the interaction of light with the microscopic inclusions within a clear stone or crystal.

Sedimentary rock: Rock formed by the weathering of substances; forming layers from accumulation of minerals and organic substances.

Semi-precious stone: Gem or gemstone used in jewelry that lacks in one or more property such as luster, hardness, or rarity that would make it a precious gemstone.

Silky (luster): Luster of minerals that have a very fine fibrous structure, causing it to display optical properties similar to silk cloth.

Specific gravity: The weight ratio of a mineral due to the density of the atomical arrangement and the heaviness of the elements it contains.

Spherulitic: Aggregate consisting of rounded, ball-like structures composed of radiating crystals.

Splintery (fracture): Fracture forming elongated splinters. All fibrous minerals fall into this category.

Stalactites: Icicle-like formations on the roof of caverns created when mineral-rich water drips down from the roof and the dissolved mineral accumulates into the icicle-like formation. May be confused with stalagmites, which are tall-domed formations on the bottom of caverns built up from the mineral-rich water depositing the dissolved mineral on the floor.

Staurolite twin: Form of penetration twinning in which two monoclinic crystals form interpenetrating twins at 90 degrees, forming a cross.

Streak: The color of a mineral's powder. A streak can be tested by rubbing a mineral against a hard, white, unglazed porcelain object (streak plate). The streak that remains is the color of the streak of the mineral.

Striations: Tiny, parallel lines or grooves seen on some crystal faces.

Structure: The form of a mineral based on the way its molecules are arranged.

Submetallic (luster): Luster of opaque to nearly opaque minerals with very good reflective properties.

Synthetic gem: Man-made gem created by using molten chemicals to solidify and form the gem.

Tabular: Crystal habit describing a flat, usually four-sided crystal where the width is at least twice the depth (thickness).

Tarnish: Oxidation occurring in some minerals that cause them to discolor when placed in certain environments.

Transparent: An object that is able to transmit light, and can clearly be seen through as if there is nothing interfering.

Translucent: Describing something that is able to transmit light, but not completely. Objects can be seen through a translucent object, but they will be unclear.

Thermoluminescence: A luminescence that results from the mild heating of a mineral. Most often seen in fluorite.

Twinning: Tendency of some crystals to intergrow in a distinct way to form a specific relationship between the crystal structures.

Uneven (fracture): Fracture that leaves a rough or irregular surface.

Vitreous (luster): Luster describing minerals with reflective properties similar to that of glass.

Vug: An open cavity or pocket in rock, often lined with crystal druses.

Waxy (luster): Luster of a mineral in which it appears to be coated by a layer of wax.

Wheat sheaf: Aggregate of compact bundles of crystals, slightly radiating and thicker at the top and the bottom than in the center. Appears in the shape of an hourglass.

Widmanstaetten lines: Etched crystal faces that are seen on some polished meteorites.

Wiry: Aggregate composed of long, slender, curvy, interwoven wires.

Resources

Book Contributors/Mineral Dealer Information

Amir Chossrow Akhavan: www.quartzpage.de

Kevin Burgart: www.curiogrove.com

Barbara Grill: www.rockshopcafe.com

Travis Hartins: Hartins Gems & Collectibles, hartinsgems@yahoo.com

William Horton: www.facebook.com/william.horton

Mike Keim: www.marinmineral.com

Kevin Kessler: www.brushymountainamethystmine.com

Klaus Klement: www.facebook.com/KandDEnterprises

Yoshihiro Kobayashi: www.facebook.com/yoshihiro.kobayashi

Lamont Latham: www.ebay.com/AZRoxz

Steve Kluck: www.facebook.com/SedonaSteven

Dr. Robert Lavinsky: The Arkenstone, www.irocks.com

Larry Michon: www.facebook.com/Larry.Michon

Suzanne Morrison: www.itsrainingrocks.com

Patti Polk: www.agategrrrl.com

Trinas Rock Shop: www.trinasrockshop.com

Online Mineral Information Resources

Mineralogy Database: www.mindat.org
  (online mineral identification database)

Mineralogical Record: www.minrec.org (online resource & magazine)

www.geology.com/minerals/ (mineral identification)

www.gia.edu (gemstone identification)

www.minerals.net

www.rockhounds.com/rockshop/mineral_id

Online Crystal Information & Metaphysical Resources

www.ancient-wisdom.com

www.cafeastrology.com

www.chakras.info

www.crystal-information.com

www.crystalvaults.com

www.crystalsrocksandgems.com

www.healing-crystals-healing-stones.com

www.heavenandearthjewelry.com

www.kacha-stones.com

www.melodycrystalsuk.co.uk

www.tokenrock.com

Mineral Digging (Fee) Opportunities

Agate, thundereggs, Oregon: richardsonrockranch.com

Amethyst quartz scepter crystals, New Mexico: brushymountainamethystmine.com

Copper minerals, Michigan: www.caledoniamine.com

Diamonds, Arkansas: www.craterofdiamondsstatepark.com

Fire agate, Arizona: www.fireagate.us/fire-agate/oatman.shtml

Fossils, crystals, Florida: www.thefortdrumcrystalmine.com

Fossils, Nebraska: www.highplainshomestead.com

Fossil fish, Wyoming: www.fossilsafari.com

Fluorescent minerals, New Jersey: sterlinghillminingmuseum.org

Gold, Alabama: www.alabamagoldcamp.com

Herkimer quartz crystals, New York: www.herkimerdiamond.com

Mica, feldspar, beryl, New Hampshire: www.rugglesmine.com

Opals, Idaho: www.spenceropalmines.com

Opals, Nevada: www.royalpeacock.com

Quartz crystal, Arkansas: www.boardcampcampground.com

Quartz crystals, South Carolina: www.dhmine.com

Quartz, beryl, tourmaline, Georgia: www.hoggmine.com

Quartz, tourmaline, beryl, Maine: www.digmainegems.com

Sapphires, Montana: www.gemmountainmt.com

Sunstone, Oregon: www.doubleeaglemine.com

Topaz, Texas: www.masontexastopaz.com

Topaz, Utah: www.topazmountainadventures.com

Tourmaline, California: www.digforgems.com

Variety of gemstones, North Carolina: www.rosecreekmine.com

Variety of gemstones, Virginia: www.morefieldgemmine.com

Gem & Mineral Shows

Gem & Lapidary Wholesalers Shows: www.glwshows.com

Martin Zinn Expositions: www.mzexpos.com

Quartzsite, AZ Pow Wow Gem & Mineral Show: www.qiaarizona.org/
POWWOW-Show.html

Tucson Gem & Mineral Show: www.tgms.org

Gem & Mineral Organizations/Clubs

American Federation of Mineralogical Societies: www.amfed.org

Fluorescent Mineral Society: www.uvminerals.org

Gem and Mineral Federation of Canada: www.gmfc.ca

Geological Society of America: www.geology.gsapubs.org
(geology magazine)

Mineralogical Society of America: www.minsocam.org

Gem & Mineral Museums in the USA

Franklin Mineral Museum: www.franklinmineralmuseum.com

Rice Museum of Rocks & Minerals: www.ricenorthwestmuseum.org

Smithsonian Mineral Sciences Collections: www.mineralsciences.
si.edu/collections.htm

Sterling Hill Mining & Mineral Museum:
www.sterlinghillminingmuseum.org

University of Arizona Mineral Museum: www.uamineralmuseum.org

Bibliography

American Geological Institute. *Dictionary of Geological Terms.* Garden City, N.Y.: Dolphin Books, 1962.

Chesterman, C.W. *Audubon Society Field Guide to North American Rocks and Minerals.* New York: Alfred A. Knopf, 1993.

Cipriani, C. and A. Borelli. *Guide to Gems and Precious Stones.* New York: Simon & Schuster, 1986.

Dake, H.C., F. Fleener, and B.H. Wilson. *Quartz Family Minerals.* New York: McGraw-Hill, 1938.

Emmons, C. and M. Fenton. *Geology Principles and Processes.* New York: McGraw-Hill, 1955.

Ford, W.E. *A Textbook of Mineralogy.* New York: John Wiley & Sons, 1966.

Gleason, S. *Ultraviolet Guide to Minerals.* North Clarendon, Vermont: Charles E. Tuttle Co., 1972.

Melody. *Love is in the Earth.* Washington: Earth-Love Publishing, 1991.

Mercier, Patricia. *The Chakra Bible.* New York: Sterling, 2007.

Mottana, A., R. Crespi and G. Liborio. *Guide to Rocks and Minerals.* New York: Simon & Schuster, 1978.

Pearl, R.M. *Cleaning and Preserving Minerals.* Colorado: Earth Science Publishing, 1973.

Pearl, R.M. *Successful Mineral Collecting & Prospecting.* New York: Bonanza Books, 1961.

Pellant, C. *Rocks & Minerals.* New York: Dorling Kindersley, 1992.

Polk, Patti. *Collecting Rocks, Gems, and Minerals* (3rd ed.). Iola, WI: Krause Publications, 2016.

Pough, F. H. *A Field Guide to Rocks & Minerals.* New York: Houghton Mifflin, 1983.

Ransom, J. *Gems and Minerals of America*. New York: Harper & Row, 1975.

Sanborn, W.B. *Handbook of Crystal & Mineral Collecting*. Baldwin Park, California: Gembooks, 1966.

Schumann, W. *Gemstones of the World*. New York: Sterling, 1977.

Simmons, Robert and Naisha Ashian. *The Book of Stones*. Vermont: Heaven & Earth Publishing, 2005.

Simpson, Liz. *Chakra Healing*. New York: Sterling Publishing, 2013.

Sinkankas, J. *Field Collecting Gemstones & Minerals*. Arizona: Geoscience Press 1988.

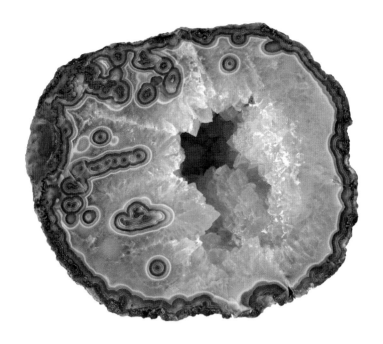

Index

A

B

C

M

macrocrystalline   8, 9, 16, 17

magnesium carbonate   92

magnetite   31, 32, 33, 127-128, 182

malachite   31, 32, 33, 48, 49, 73, 86, 91, 129, 198, 200

metamorphic rock   15, 16-17

millerite   130

mimetite   131-132, 149, 227

Mohs scale   17-18

moldavite   133

muscovite   32, 58, 125, 134-135

N

natrolite   32, 136, 137

neptunite   53, 137

numerical properties   36-38

   number 1   36, 49, 51, 55, 77, 81, 100, 108, 116, 134, 148, 194, 218, 224, 225

   number 2   36, 42, 48, 59, 69, 82, 86, 94, 96, 105, 108, 113, 114, 122, 216, 218, 219, 220

   number 3   37, 56, 57, 70, 82, 90, 92, 122, 146, 203, 215, 219

   number 4   37, 45, 56, 83, 87, 99, 109, 110, 120, 123, 127, 130, 131, 189, 191, 197, 211, 218, 219, 231, 232

   number 5   37, 57, 61, 66, 73, 89, 98, 107, 139, 143, 193, 200, 206, 218, 220, 229

   number 6   37, 71, 84, 99, 108, 136, 139, 200, 204, 213, 219

   number 7   37, 40, 76, 79, 83, 85, 93, 99, 101, 108, 109, 125, 137, 138, 139, 141, 145, 149, 198, 200, 205, 209, 227

   number 8   38, 55, 58, 64, 67, 74, 91, 126, 187, 195, 207, 221

   number 9   38, 43, 46, 53, 63, 97, 118, 129, 133, 142, 215, 222

   number 22   98, 104

   number 33   90, 118, 208

   number 44   100, 111, 196

O

okenite   138

olivine   139-140

P

pendant   14, 27

pendulum   6, 29

petalite   32, 141, 204

phenakite   142

prehnite   32, 45, 89, 138, 143-144, 208

proustite   145

pyrite   64, 83, 93, 146-147, 178, 181, 182, 201

pyrolusite   32, 148, 182

pyromorphite   131, 149, 227

Q

U

ulexite 32, 76, 221

V

vanadinite 85, 131, 149, 222-223, 227

vivianite 224

W

wand 12, 28

wavellite 225-226

wulfenite 85, 131, 222, 227-228

Z

zinc carbonate 198

zincite 12, 229-230

zircon 32, 230

zodiac signs 31-33

   Aquarius 33, 35, 48, 51, 59, 66, 97, 98, 105, 108, 109, 119, 127, 134, 145, 196, 197, 224, 225

   Aries 31, 35, 55, 56, 76, 85, 89, 90, 92, 109, 111, 114, 119, 123, 127, 133,

149, 203, 208, 220

   Cancer 32, 35, 64, 82, 99, 100, 107, 108, 116, 133, 136, 197

   Capricorn 33, 35, 46, 67, 86, 96, 101, 104, 105, 122, 127, 129, 131, 194, 207, 219

   Gemini 32, 35, 43, 45, 55, 56, 67, 73, 82, 94, 100, 125, 142, 191, 201, 219, 221, 232

   Leo 32, 35, 57, 71, 74, 82, 87, 90, 99, 100, 105, 107, 113, 134, 139, 141, 145, 146, 148, 149, 189, 205, 209, 215, 231

   Libra 32, 35, 45, 56, 57, 79, 92, 99, 100, 120, 123, 126, 143, 193, 200, 216, 219, 229

   Pisces 33, 35, 42, 55, 93, 101, 116, 136, 137, 198, 206, 215

   Sagittarius 32, 35, 49, 63, 77, 79, 81, 83, 91, 122, 125, 138, 139, 149, 203, 211, 213, 215, 218, 220, 227, 231

   Scorpio 32, 35, 58, 82, 91, 99, 129, 130, 136, 139, 187, 189, 204, 205, 207, 218

   Taurus 31, 35, 55, 56, 61, 73, 77, 79, 86, 90, 96, 118, 123, 191, 195, 205, 219, 229

   Virgo 32, 35, 40, 53, 69, 70, 73, 82, 84, 86, 96, 98, 105, 110, 127, 138, 139, 198, 215, 319, 222, 231

zoisite 32, 94, 232-233